WENDY ARNOLD

The Historic Hotels of London

A Select Guide

With 123 color photographs by
ROBIN MORRISON

Holt, Rinehart and Winston
New York

For Ian and Nikki, Robin and Kim, and Tiffany

*On the jacket: a table in The Dorchester's Terrace Restaurant.
See p. 39.*

*Frontispiece: a doorman in splendid livery stands on the steps of
the Arlington Street entrance to The Ritz, ready to greet visitors.
See p. 77.*

*Opposite: the Chinese Room in Blakes is typical of this hotel's
richly decorated sophisticated interiors. See p. 19.*

Published in the United States by
Holt, Rinehart and Winston, 383 Madison Avenue,
New York, New York 10017.

Library of Congress Cataloging in Publication Data

Arnold, Wendy.
    The historic hotels of London.

    Includes index.
    1. Hotels, taverns, etc.—England—London—
Directories. I. Title.
TX910.G7A663   1986   647′.9442101   85-27074
ISBN: 0-03-007303-0

First American Edition

Designer: Geoffrey Penna
Printed in Hong Kong

10 9 8 7 6 5 4 3 2 1

ISBN 0-03-007303-0

Contents

Preface

Tower Bridge and the Thames, seen through a window in 'Captain Webb', a Victorian barge converted into a luxury hotel. See p. 29.

London's historic hotels are as fascinating as the city itself. On a wave of nostalgia for times past many have been lovingly restored, and have acquired a magnificent new lease of life. Millions have been spent to recreate the splendor that was theirs in the early days of the century. Marble foyers gleam, crystal chandeliers glitter, fine antique furniture once more graces the high-ceilinged drawing rooms and lavish bedrooms, splendid chefs prepare delicious dishes, attentive staff are alert to every whim, doormen in well-cut livery doff their top hats, and the Rolls is sent to meet you at the airport. For those seeking less palatial comfort, there are Georgian mansions in quiet streets, whose owners themselves will welcome you, and even a luxuriously appointed Victorian barge which ferries fortunate guests languorously down the Royal Road of the Thames, while they enjoy afternoon tea.

Thirty years of living abroad, including four heady years in the USA accompanying my husband's oil-community flittings about the world – flying off by executive jet to Venezuela for a cocktail party or to Cairo for a consultation at a moment's notice – meant staying in many hotels. The modern ones, so useful to businessmen on a rapid visit, are confusingly alike. You wake to the same décor in Dubai and Dallas, Mexico and Monaco. After investigating England's country hotels for my first book, *The Historic Country Hotels of England*, we settled in rural Hampshire, England, where we have been visited by American friends who enjoyed the selection of country hotels, but now wanted to know whether hotels of similar individuality and excellence could be found in London.

After six months of careful research, I narrowed down the choice to the eighty which sounded most civilized, visited them all, and stayed at those I found most appetizing. It was interesting to compare the glowing promises of the brochures with the reality. Since I accept no hospitality or free meals, am paid no expenses, arrive unannounced, and only reveal my purpose in staying *after* paying the bill, I receive an unvarnished impression of the hotel's attitude to guests. London prices, I found, marvellously concentrated the mind, and sharpened an awareness of, and outrage at, poor food, ungracious service, and shoddy décor. When faced with any of these, I informed the manager, and left.

Happily, however, I found that there are superb hotels in London, which will welcome you warmly, make sure you have everything you want, treat you as a person, not just as a room number, and will even turn down your bed at night. The fact that they also have splendid historic buildings, delicious food, attentive service, spotless rooms, elegant décor, and highly trained and efficient management is a bonus.

Of the many places to stay in London, these are the ones I would recommend to my friends, and to which I would most happily return.

General Information

Preparation Booking as many months in advance as possible is essential for all these establishments. June and July are London's peak tourist months. The map overleaf and the notes after each entry give a general idea of which hotels are most convenient for shopping, antique hunting, theaters, museums, or the City. If you travel with a great deal of luggage and require a specially large room, or with friends who want identical accommodation to yours, if you cannot manage stairs, prefer modern to antique furniture, want a six-feet-wide double bed, airconditioning, and a shower, be certain to mention this when booking. In historic hotels nothing is standardized, which is their charm.

Terms Since prices fluctuate, I have divided the hotels into three broad categories based on what they charge for two people sharing a double room for one night, including the obligatory 15% government tax (VAT), the usual 10% service charge, and the cost of a continental breakfast. Hotels do not always include these in their advertised charge. (The dollar equivalent is based on a rate of exchange of £1 = $1.40.)

> *Accommodation for two*
> Moderate £50–100 (approx. $70–140)
> Medium £101–140 (approx. $141–196)
> Expensive £141–200 (approx. $197–280)

This does not include extras such as drinks, telephone calls, or (except when stated) full English breakfast. The cost of other meals is quoted separately:

> *Meals for two*
> Moderate £10–29 (approx. $14–41)
> Medium £30–49 (approx. $42–69)
> Expensive £50–80 (approx. $70–112)

This represents the average price of an *à la carte* meal without wine, but including tax, service at 10%, and any cover charge. Most restaurants provide a fixed-price menu in addition, and I have mentioned if this is available. Special low-price pre-theater suppers and out-of-season or weekend reductions for accommodation are occasionally offered. Enquire when booking.

Private homes The owners of private homes receiving guests that I have included belong to organizations which inspect them and centralize bookings. Contact: In the English Manner, Mawley House, Quenington, Nr. Cirencester, Gloucs. GL7 5BH [tel: (0285) 75267/telex: (851) 449703] or At Home, The Stone House, Great Gransden, Sandy, Beds. SG19 3AF [tel: (076) 777025/telex: 81574 GTACAM G AT HOME], both of which will make bookings for you. Wolsey Lodges, 17 Chapel Street, Bildeston, Ipswich, Suffolk IP7 7EP [tel: (0449) 740609/telex: 987703 EATB] and The Heritage Circle, Burghope Manor, Winsley, Nr. Bradford-on-Avon, Wilts. [tel: (022122) 3557/telex: 444337 ACTBUS G HERITAGE] will either book for you, or allow you to book your own choice from their brochure.

Transport Parking is difficult in London. I have noted if it is provided by hotels; if it is not, I have indicated where it is available close by. This is usually in a fee-paying National Car Park (NCP). The drivers of London's black taxicabs undergo extensive training lasting up to 2 years, are given detailed examinations of their local knowledge, are checked by doctors and police before receiving licenses, and must by law maintain their vehicles both inside and out. Minicab drivers are usually unlicensed and unchecked. Underground (tube) trains are usually the fastest way to get around, but can spring nasty surprises such as out-of-action moving stairs and lengthy passageways linking different lines. Red London buses give excellent views of the city from their top deck, but move slowly in rush hours. Concessionary passes for varying periods on tube and bus offer a bargain to dedicated sightseers.

Sightseeing *What's On?* and *Time Out*, two widely available weekly magazines, give general information on theaters, cinemas, restaurants, and other entertainments. *Historic Houses, Castles and Gardens in Great Britain and Ireland*, published in the U.K. annually, gives details of opening times and admission charges; Michelin's Green London Guide is very comprehensive and grades the appeal of things to see. *Inner London in Super Scale* by the Geographers' A-Z Map Co. has the most easily readable maps and gazetteer. *Eating Out in London*, published by *Time Out* magazine, is a very detailed restaurant guide. All are available from most London bookstores and newsstands.

A footnote I am confident that the owners and managers of the establishments I have selected will ensure that guests are treated with courtesy and consideration at all times. It helps them to be told *personally* of any difficulties – or indeed of any particularly good points – about their hotels. I too should be most grateful to hear about them, care of the publishers.

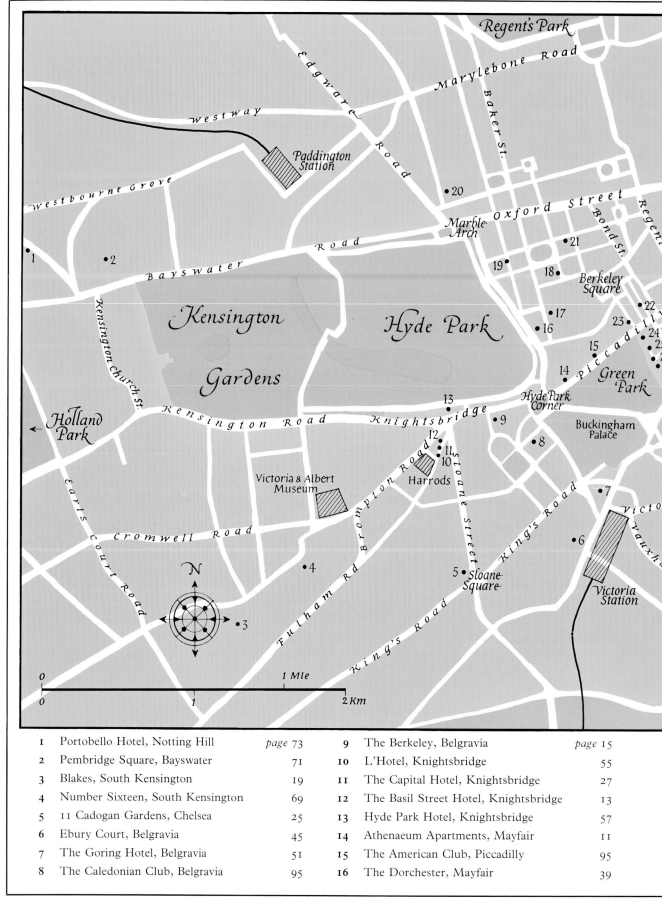

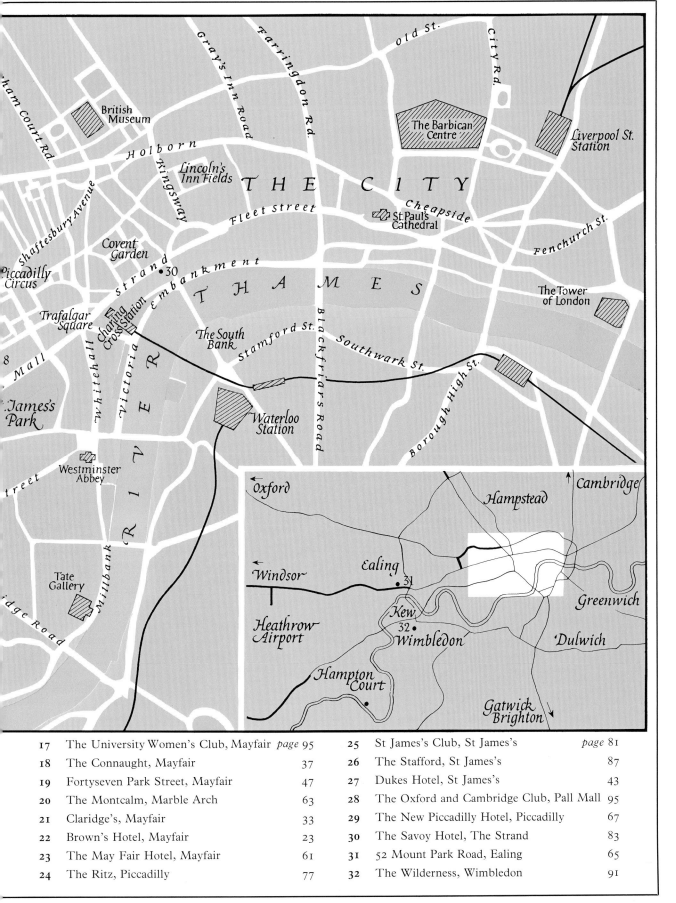

Athenaeum Apartments

Edwardian seclusion

Mayfair, now London's most fashionable district, was until the end of the 18th century a thoroughly disreputable area of open fields. A fair was held there under charter from James II, "on the first day of May, to continue for fourteen days after, yearly, for ever." To see mountebanks and jugglers, conjurers and puppet shows, fire-eaters and prize-fighters, tigers and elephants, tightrope walkers and ladies of ill repute, a great noisy drunken crowd gathered there. Pockets were picked, fortunes were lost on the gaming table, and illegal marriages were performed in a chapel by a reprobate clergyman at any hour of the day or night, no questions asked. With the building of Berkeley and Grosvenor Squares, and of stately mansions along Piccadilly and Park Lane, the fields began to disappear and the nobility started to complain about the noise and disorderly conduct of the riff-raff. In 1809 the May Fair was finally suppressed, leaving only its name, but Shepherd Market, where the crowds made their purchases, still remains, a fascinating jumble of narrow streets and ancient buildings.

Just a step away, in a row of neat, turn-of-the-century houses with bay windows, iron railings, and colorful windowboxes, are the Athenaeum Apartments. Immaculately maintained, luxuriously comfortable, they are an alternative to a hotel suite and provide the added advantages of privacy and a fully equipped modern all-electric kitchen. A jogging map is provided for the athletic, since Green Park is just the other side of Piccadilly, and tracksuits are available on request. Buckingham Palace, the lake and gardens of St James's Park, and many of London's most elegant shops and restaurants are close by.

My apartment had its own hallway, impeccable pine kitchen, and gleaming modern bathroom. The bedroom, furnished in toning shades of rust and beige, was equipped with a six-feet-wide double bed, prettily draped with curtains in a delicate leaf pattern, a deep walk-in clothes closet, color television, direct-dial phone, and a comfortable velvet armchair. The spacious living room had fabrics with an antique pattern of birds and plants, dining table and chairs, and a further phone and television.

The apartments belong to, and are at the back of, the excellent and attentive Athenaeum Hotel on Piccadilly, which provides everything offered to its own guests except room service and will stock refrigerators in the apartments on request. It has a panelled bar specializing in Scottish malt whiskies, a charming restaurant, and delicious afternoon teas, all adding to the enjoyment of a stay in this exclusive home from home.

Opposite: top, an elegant sitting room in one of the apartments; bottom, the dining room in the adjoining Athenaeum Hotel. Above: a king-sized bed in an apartment bedroom.

ATHENAEUM APARTMENTS, Down Street, W1V oBJ. For booking, contact Athenaeum Hotel, 116 Piccadilly, W1V oBJ. **Map reference** 14. **Tel.** Athenaeum Hotel: (o1) 499 3464. **Telex** 261589. **Owners** Rank Hotels. **Manager** Nicholas Rettie. **Open** All year. **Rooms** 40 double-bedroom apartments, 3 two-bedroom apartments, all with bathroom (including shower), kitchen, color TV, 2 or 3 direct-dial or operator phones, radio. **Facilities** Entry phone, elevator, porter service, Mon.–Fri. maid service, same-day laundry/drycleaning/valeting service (weekdays only), baby sitting. In hotel: bar, lounge, restaurant, 3 private reception suites, beauty salon, in-house nurse, hospitality service to meet/greet and advise first-time visitors, photocopying and document delivery service, safe.

Restrictions No dogs (guidedogs excepted). **Terms** Medium. **Lunch** (in hotel) Medium. Medium fixed-price menu. **Dinner** (in hotel) Expensive. Moderate fixed-price pre-theater suppers. **Credit cards** All major cards. **Nearest tube station** Green Park, $\frac{1}{4}$ mile. **Hotel parking** Yes, but limited. **Local eating** The Dorchester Grill and Terrace Restaurant (see p. 39); The Greenhouse, 27a Hay's Mews, W1; The Ritz (see p. 77); fashionable snacks at Hard Rock Café, 150 Old Park Lane, W1. **Local shopping** Bond Street; Burlington Arcade; Fortnum and Mason's and other Piccadilly stores; Cork Street commercial art galleries. **Local interest** Green Park; Buckingham Palace, Apsley House (Duke of Wellington museum) and Hyde Park; Royal Academy; Museum of Mankind.

Old-world charm

The impressive room to the left of the entrance in the Basil Street Hotel started life as a booking hall for the underground railway. By the time the Taylor family bought the hotel in 1919, this had become an elegant ballroom, much in demand in an era when the landed gentry came to London to have their daughters presented at Court, and stayed on for the London season of parties and balls. Today it is a club, set aside for lady guests of the hotel and country members coming up for the day to shop at Harrods, which is just at the other end of Basil Street.

Narrow marble steps lead to a half gallery, where you sign in. A friendly reception girl will take you up in the one tiny elevator to long, narrow corridors, off which are the comfortable and surprisingly quiet bedrooms, all with fine bedlinen. The pine-panelled or tiled bathrooms have excellent showers, and many are very large, since they were originally single bedrooms.

The hotel has a gracious Edwardian entrance hall, with an oriental carpet, potted palms, fresh flowers, and a graceful staircase leading up to a large lounge, where comfortable, chintz-covered easy chairs in well-spaced groups create a club-like atmosphere. A bell on the wall can be rung to summon a waiter to bring morning coffee, afternoon tea, or drinks. A long gallery, with windowed alcoves on one side, each with a writing desk, has large antique vases, paintings on glass, polished woodblock floors, and dark red and blue carpets. It leads to a stately panelled restaurant, painted pale green and candlelit at night, which serves traditional English food. A coffee shop, "Upstairs," offers buffet meals, snacks, and sandwiches to guests, shoppers, and local office-workers; "Downstairs" is a cellar wine-bar for those not wanting a formal restaurant meal.

People enjoy The Basil. An American Ladies' Club was happily lunching there at a long table beside mine, and I was nearly swamped on the stairs by an eager rush of small girls dressed as clowns and clutching elegantly wrapped gifts, coming to a party. In the words of Stephen Korany, General Manager for more than 30 years, there is something special about a place that has been in the same family for 75 years. Although not the most grandiose hotel in London, The Basil is certainly one of the best loved.

Opposite: the main staircase, which leads up to the Lounge.
Above: an inviting easy chair in a corner of this comfortable hotel.

THE BASIL STREET HOTEL, Basil Street, SW3 1AH. **Map reference** 12. **Tel.** (01) 581 3311. **Telex** 28379. **Owner** Private partnership. **General Manager** Stephen Korany. **Open** All year. **Rooms** 62 single, 41 double, most with bathroom which has shower over tub, and hairdryer, all with color TV, direct-dial phone, and radio. **Facilities** 24-hr. room service, elevator, 24-hr. laundry/drycleaning/valeting service (weekdays only), ladies' club room, lounge, restaurant, writing rooms, private reception and conference rooms, safe. **Restrictions** No dogs in public rooms. **Terms** Moderate. **Lunch/Dinner** (in restaurant) Moderate. Only fixed-price menu at lunchtime. **Credit cards** All major cards. **Nearest tube station** Knightsbridge, 150 yds. **Hotel parking** No. NCP in Pavilion Road, SW1. **Local eating** Capital Hotel and Le Metro, Basil Street, SW3 (see pp. 27 and 55); Harrods' snackbars; Bendick's and GTC, Sloane Street, SW1, for light meals. **Local shopping** Harrods, Harvey Nichols, Scotch House, and other Knightsbridge stores; Peter Jones; King's Road and Sloane Street boutiques. **Local interest** Royal Albert Hall; Hyde Park and Kensington Gardens for jogging, riding, and boating; Natural History, Science, Geological, and Victoria & Albert museums.

The Berkeley

Belgravia

Formal comforts

Apsley House, on Hyde Park Corner, has the impressive address "Number One, London." It is still the town house of the Dukes of Wellington and the first duke's soldiers, who fought at the Battle of Waterloo, used to drill on a barracks square opposite, where The Berkeley now stands.

The hotel's owners, the Savoy group, boldly moved name, traditions, silver, linen, fireplaces, wood panelling, antique clocks, pictures, and a complete room by famous architect Sir Edwin Lutyens from the original Mayfair site to an entirely new airconditioned, double-glazed, centrally-heated building with a penthouse swimming pool and subterranean garage. Corridor carpets were specially woven from a 13th-century embroidery design discovered in a French cathedral and Michael Inchbold and other top designers were called in to create elegant private reception rooms and suites. Nobody knew whether the clientèle of the old hotel, whose loyalty had been built up over a hundred years, would approve. They did.

There is nothing of the brash modern hotel about this new Berkeley. Uniformed doormen greet you politely, porters efficiently whisk your luggage away, and elegantly clothed, very correct young managers formally dressed in black jackets first conduct you to an antique desk to sign in, then escort you to your room or suite, to make certain that it is to your satisfaction. The bedrooms, each of which has its own anteroom, are not standardized in any way. Some are traditional, with dark wood panelling, velvet upholstery, antique furniture, and chandeliers, others are modern, with light chintzes and prints. All have modern bathrooms ranging from the large to the enormous.

Rooms on the top floor have little balconies overlooking London, and are near the elegant penthouse swimming pool, which has its own restaurant, a flower-bedecked sunning area, and a sliding roof for inclement weather. For dinner there is a choice between the main restaurant, newly redecorated, and the elegant Buttery, where I enjoyed a delicious meal. The selection of *hors d'oeuvres* was outstanding, and rack of lamb with fresh vegetables, followed by mango icecream, were superb. There is an encyclopedic wine list, compiled with great expertise. After a luxuriously comfortable night, Sunday morning brought a brief but penetrating peal of bells from St Paul's church next door, and an excellent breakfast, served on pretty blue-green Wedgwood china. The Berkeley is a hotel which is at the same time traditionally historic and conveniently modern. A remarkable achievement.

Opposite: in the restaurant diners can enjoy the trompe l'oeil view of Apsley House while sampling a delicious dessert from the trolley. A typically appealing bedroom is shown above; overleaf is the magnificent penthouse pool, which has a roof that is slid open in fine weather.

THE BERKELEY, Wilton Place, SW1X 7RL. **Map reference** 9. **Tel.** (01) 235 6000. **Telex** 919252. **Owners** The Savoy Hotel plc. **General Manager** Stefano Sebastiani. **Open** All year. **Rooms** 130 rooms, 25 suites, all with bathroom (including shower), foyers, airconditioning, doubleglazing, color TV, radio. **Facilities** 24-hr. room service, maid, valet, and waiter service, 2-day or express same-day drycleaning/laundry/valeting services, elevators, restaurant and Buttery, bar, Lutyens Room, ballroom, reception rooms, swimming pool, saunas, massage, beauty treatments, ladies' and gentlemen's hairdressers, baby sitting, safe, cinema, flower shop, garage, hotel representatives at Heathrow and Southampton to assist arrival and departure, picnic hampers by arrangement. **Restrictions** No dogs. **Terms** Expensive. **Lunch/Dinner** (in both restaurant and Buttery) Expensive. **Credit cards** All major cards. **Nearest tube station** Hyde Park Corner, 100 yds. **Hotel parking** Yes (capacity 50 cars). **Local eating** The Capital Hotel and Le Metro, Basil Street, SW3 (see pp. 27 and 55), The Dorchester (see p. 39). **Local shopping** Harrods and other Knightsbridge stores; Sloane Street and King's Road boutiques. **Local interest** Hyde Park; Buckingham Palace and St James's Palace; Royal Albert Hall; Natural History, Science, Geological, and Victoria & Albert museums; Duke of Wellington Museum in Apsley House.

Fashionable flair

Blakes shows just what exciting things can be done to a row of fairly ordinary 19th-century houses. A new foyer has been added, but the rest of the hotel is a fascinating blend of modern and Victorian. In the reception area, a vast square umbrella stands over the stairs leading down to the restaurant. A mountain of the sort of luggage that accompanied a 19th-century explorer stands as though waiting for Stanley's bearers to lift it to their shoulders and set off in search of Livingstone. It is topped by a cage containing a pretty pink and green parakeet that I thought was stuffed, until it startled me by moving. There is a background color scheme of black and white lightened by dove-gray and refreshing moss green. The reception girls are cool, elegant, and extremely efficient, the porter cheerful and friendly.

This fashionable haunt of media people has the faintly world-weary air of those accustomed to the presence of the famous and the wealthy. Guests frequently arrive at strange hours of the night, having flown in from California, or having just finished a lengthy recording session. Whatever meal is currently offered in the restaurant can also be served in the rooms, supported by a most comprehensive 24-hour room-service menu. The selection is tailored to the tastes of a sophisticated international clientèle and offers bortsch, blini, sashimi, satay, szechwan duck, and coffee with cardamon, as well as roast lamb, fudge cake, bacon-lettuce-and-tomato toasted sandwiches, live yoghurt with banana, wheat germ, and clover honey. The mirror-lined restaurant is modern, with round tables covered with black or white cloths alternately. Low square glass vases stuffed with bright lilies add splashes of color.

Pre-dinner drinks and after-dinner coffee are served in the Chinese Room, where soft squishy chairs line the walls round a vast square table piled

high with art books and magazines. Talk tends to be of contracts and festivals, success at Cannes, or returning to location in Tunisia. With difficulty I stopped myself greeting as an old friend somebody whose face was familiar to me only because it appeared daily on my television screen.

The stylish bedrooms, reached by an elevator for the weary, are totally different from one another. Mine had vast mirrors, white paintwork, green and white lattice-patterned drapes and bedcover, a large potted palm, and a gleamingly clean gray and white bathroom with big white towels. Storage space was ample. This is a sophisticated, laid-back, and efficiently run hotel of great personality.

Opposite: two glimpses of the stylish bedrooms; the model of Marlene Dietrich (above) is on the bar. The glamorous interiors overleaf are, left, a bathroom and, right, the Chinese Room, where guests relax after dinner.

BLAKES, 33 Roland Gardens, SW7 3PF. **Map reference** 3. **Tel.** (01) 370 6701. **Telex** 8813500. **Owner** Anouska Hempel Weinberg. **Managing Director** Leonard Burrows. **Open** All year. **Rooms** 10 single, 13 double, 30 luxury doubles/suites, 12 apartments, all with bathroom (including shower), color TV, direct-dial phone, mini-bar, safe. **Facilities** Elevator, restaurant, Chinese Room, bar, 24-hr. room service, safe, same-day laundry/dry-cleaning/valeting service (weekdays only), sauna. **Restrictions** No dogs. **Terms** Medium. **Lunch/Dinner** Expensive. **Credit cards** All major cards. **Nearest tube station** South Kensington, $\frac{1}{2}$ mile. **Hotel parking** No. Nearest is at Gloucester Hotel, 4 Harrington Gardens, SW7. **Local eating** Small local restaurants only; across the river in Battersea is L'Arlequin, 123 Queenstown Road, SW8 – my favorite restaurant in England. **Local shopping** King's Road and Fulham Road boutiques; Harrods and Knightsbridge stores (1 mile). **Local interest** Kensington Gardens and Kensington Palace; Royal Albert Hall; Natural History, Science, Geological, and Victoria & Albert museums.

Brown's Hotel

Mayfair

Traditional excellence

When visiting Brown's Hotel, Queen Victoria used to sit in the blue velvet chair with gilded legs and arms that is proudly preserved, together with an identical second chair (for Prince Albert, perhaps?), in a curtained alcove at the top of the stairs. In front of them is a fine ornate antique desk, at which author Rudyard Kipling worked when staying here. Over the years many crowned heads and world leaders have selected Brown's rather than one of London's more imposing establishments, perhaps because, being made up of twelve small Georgian and Victorian houses, it feels much more like a private residence than a hotel. The reception rooms are low ceilinged and wood panelled, with alcoves and antiques, fat velvet chairs, and plenty of fresh flowers. Each bedroom has an individual character, with pretty wallpaper, toning bedcovers and paintwork, ample clothes space, a good bathroom, mini-bar, and color television; some have airconditioning.

Although bought several years ago by Trusthouse Forte, Brown's has wisely been allowed to keep its own traditions of attentive personal service, established in 1837 by James Brown, a retired gentleman's gentleman, in one little house in Dover Street. With the assistance of his wife, a former lady's maid to Lord Byron's widow, he built up a reputation for such excellent service that another four adjoining houses were purchased, catering admirably to the influx of visitors that came to the Great Exhibition of 1851 in nearby Hyde Park. His successor introduced all sorts of modern marvels to the hotel: electricity, fixed baths with piped water, and telephones – Alexander Graham Bell made one of Britain's first phone calls from Brown's. Theodore Roosevelt was married from the hotel, and his cousin Franklin stayed here for part of his honeymoon.

When I first knew Brown's, it was a quiet, traditional, slightly faded place where nicely-brought-up girls from the country might stay respectably, and where fires were still lit for guests in the bedroom grates. Now it is elegant and impeccable, and many of the voices overheard at the fashionable afternoon teatime are transatlantic, exclaiming with pleasure over the pink wild-rose-patterned Wedgwood china, and the well-provisioned three-tiered cake stands. Dinner in the delightful panelled restaurant attracts an even more international clientèle and was equally delicious and pleasantly served; the selection of wines is perfectly balanced, from the unassuming to the outstanding, and is sensibly priced. I think that James Brown would be very pleased to see how, after a century and a half, the highest standards are still maintained in his hotel.

Brown's is famous for its afternoon teas (opposite); one of its attractive and very comfortable bedrooms is shown above.

BROWN'S HOTEL, Albemarle and Dover Streets, W1A 4SW. **Map reference** 22. **Tel.** (01) 493 6020. **Telex** 28686. **Owners** Trusthouse Forte. **General Manager** Bruce Banister. **Open** All year. **Rooms** 22 single, 113 double, 12 suites, all with bathroom (including shower), color TV, most with mini-bar, direct-dial phone, some with airconditioning. **Facilities** Elevators, restaurant, bar, lounge, safe-deposit boxes, after-theater suppers available in lounge, 36-hr. or same-day express cleaning/laundry/pressing. **Restrictions** Dogs by arrangement only. **Terms** Medium. **Lunch** Medium. Medium fixed-price menu. **Dinner** Expensive. Medium fixed-price menu. **Credit cards** All major cards. **Nearest tube station** Green Park, 300 yds. **Hotel parking** No. NCP in Carrington Street, W1 (Shepherd Market), hotel will take car to and from car park for small charge. **Local eating** The Ritz (see p. 77); Fortnum and Mason's and Simpson's, Piccadilly; The Connaught (see p. 37); Westbury Hotel, Conduit Street, W1. **Local Shopping** Bond Street; Piccadilly stores; Jermyn Street; Burlington Arcade; Cork Street commercial art galleries; Regent Street stores. **Local interest** Royal Academy; Museum of Mankind; Green Park and Buckingham Palace.

11 Cadogan Gardens

A stylish town house

Staying at 11 Cadogan Gardens is like visiting very English, very aristocratic friends who have unavoidably been called away, but have kindly left you the use of their fully staffed house in town. From the outside there is nothing to indicate that this gabled, red-brick mansion is other than a private residence. Ring the bell and a porter in a stiffly starched white jacket instantly appears to take your suitcases. You are greeted in the oak-panelled hall, which has beautiful arrangements of fresh flowers, and you sign the Visitors' Book. Kind enquiries are made as to whether you would perhaps like a cup of tea, a sandwich, or light meal. An elevator carries you up past the oak-bannistered staircase, whose walls are hung with portraits in oils, and you are guided through a series of corridors to your room. Having made certain that it is to your satisfaction, enquired the hour at which you wish breakfast to be brought to you, and encouraged you to leave your shoes outside the door at night to be polished, the management leaves you in peace.

Do not expect designer décor or opulent bathrooms. In the faintly haphazard way that all connoisseurs of the English way of life will instantly recognize and appreciate, excellent antiques, quite ordinary oak and mahogany furniture, elegant fabrics, cozy chairs, charming Victoriana, and plenty of magazines and books are assembled as in a family home. There is a formal drawing room, but no dining room. The range of bedrooms includes tiny single rooms, small suites, and some enormous double rooms. The splendid Garden Suite has its own door on to the street, two vast bedrooms, a huge drawing room with elaborate fireplace and club fender, and an air of sedate distinction that makes it eminently suitable for the international antique dealers by whom it is often selected.

In the morning, breakfast trays rattle up from the kitchens below in the dumb waiter. Breakfast is well presented, with heavy linen napery, a large glass of freshly squeezed orange juice, fresh fruit, croissants, a large jug of excellent coffee, and, if you wish, kippers or bacon and egg. Service is quiet, efficient, and unobtrusive.

Arrangements can be made for visits to hairdresser, theater, or restaurant. The Rolls and Camilo the chauffeur are at your disposal for journeys to and from the airport, or for sightseeing or shopping expeditions. On a fine day a porter will carry a deckchair into the private garden for you to sit in peaceful, leafy tranquillity. On leaving, you will stop at the manager's office to settle your account, and to leave something for the staff, since direct tipping is not customary here. A stay at 11 Cadogan Gardens is a memorable experience.

The interiors have an elegant domestic atmosphere: there are pretty fabrics in the bedrooms (above), antiques in the sitting room (opposite, bottom), and oil paintings on the stairs. The exterior view is from Cadogan Gardens.

11 CADOGAN GARDENS, Sloane Square, SW3 2RJ. **Map reference** 5. **Tel.** (01) 730 3426. **Telex** 881 3318. **Owners** 11 Cadogan Gardens Ltd. **Managers** Mark Fresson, Alan Eyers, Miss Clare Armstrong, Miss Elizabeth Radley Smith. **Open** All year. **Rooms** 60 rooms, 4 suites, Garden Suite. All with bathroom (including shower), direct-dial phone. Optional TV at extra charge. **Facilities** Drawing room, elevator, access to private garden, 24-hr. laundry and drycleaning, conference/private dining room, chauffeur-driven Rolls or estate car. **Restrictions** No dogs or children. **Terms** Medium. **Lunch/Dinner** No, but light meals available from room service; special dinner parties by arrangement. **Credit cards** No, but traveller's checks and foreign currency accepted. **Nearest tube station** Sloane Square, ¼ mile. **Hotel parking** No. Nearest is under Carlton Tower Hotel, Cadogan Place, SW1. **Local eating** Snacks at Bendick's and GTC, Sloane Street, SW3; Le Metro and Capital Hotel, Basil Street, SW3 (see pp. 55 and 27); Ma Cuisine, 113 Walton Street, SW3; Walton's, 121 Walton Street, SW3; Ménage à Trois, 15 Beauchamp Place, SW3 (just starters and desserts); The English Garden, 10 Lincoln Street, SW3. **Local Shopping** King's Road boutiques; Harrods and other Knightsbridge stores; Peter Jones, Sloane Square. **Local interest** Chelsea Hospital and its gardens (annual flower show in May); Chelsea Physic Garden; National Army Museum; Royal Court Theatre and King's Road.

Gourmet sophistication

The Capital Hotel is a gem. Hidden down a quiet little street beside Harrods, in the heart of fashionable Knightsbridge, it has no vast echoing marble halls and no serried ranks of minions, but attentive porters appear at your taxi door when you arrive, and desk staff and managers are both welcoming and efficient. The hotel's Edwardian wing was once Squires Hotel, which flourished in the 1920s. Its wide and richly carved staircase, hidden away behind the snug little dark green sitting room, ascends to a maze of narrow corridors which lead to 10 bedrooms, all different in shape and size. There is also an elevator serving all bedrooms, including 50 in a modern, more standardized wing.

Owner David Levin, and brilliant designer Nina Campbell, whose elegant décor at Hambleton Hall hotel in Leicestershire I greatly admire, have combined every thoughtful feature one would hope to find in a modern hotel with the beautiful fabrics, mellow wood, green plants, fresh flowers, paintings, and furniture one would expect only in an elegant private house. My airconditioned room in the Edwardian wing was furnished in creams and blues, with touches of terracotta. What seemed to be well-stocked library shelves opened to reveal a deep, walk-in, well-lit hanging and shelved closet, with extra storage space above for suitcases. The glamorous bathroom, most generously equipped with toiletries, had an excellent shower and towelling robes.

The Capital's French restaurant and bar have a Parisian élan and style that is matched by the menu. Calves' liver served on an attractively variegated salad with asparagus vinaigrette, red mullet with a delicate sauce St Jacques and tiny green beans and new potatoes, a passion-fruit crème brulée with a

subtly sharp flavor, handmade chocolates proffered on a large silver tray, and freshly made tuilles aux amandes with the coffee could not have been more delicious – a fact well known to London's gourmets, so restaurant and hotel booking should be simultaneous. An informed choice of wines complements the superb cuisine.

David Levin has turned the house next door to The Capital into six compact luxury apartments, complete with galley kitchens, and one door nearer to Harrods are L'Hotel and Le Metro (see p. 55), for those paying a rapid visit to London. His restaurant specializing in English dishes, The Greenhouse in Mayfair's Hay's Mews, completes a small empire which is the daily concern of its dedicated owner. He has created a happy *esprit de corps* among his staff, and a feeling of great contentment in his constantly returning guests.

Opposite: the hotel's beautiful restaurant is a famous rendezvous for gourmets. Above is one of the bedrooms designed by Nina Campbell; the bookshelves conceal closets.

THE CAPITAL HOTEL, 22 Basil Street, SW3 1AT. **Map reference** 11. **Tel.** (01) 589 5171. **Telex** 919042. **Owner** David Levin. **Manager** Keith M. Williams. **Open** All year. **Rooms** In hotel: 20 single, 30 double, 10 suites; also 5 apartments and 1 penthouse; all with bathroom (including shower), color TV, direct-dial phone, airconditioning. **Facilities** Sitting room, bar, restaurant, Eaton and Cadogan suites for private dining, parties, or meetings, 24-hr. room service, same-day laundry/drycleaning/valeting/pressing service, secretarial service. **Restrictions** No dogs in public rooms. **Terms** Medium. **Lunch** Medium. Medium fixed-price menu. **Dinner** Expensive. Medium fixed-price menu. **Credit cards** All major cards. **Nearest tube station** Knightsbridge, 50 yds. **Hotel parking** Yes, for 12 cars. Also NCP in Pavilion Road, SW1. **Local eating** Le Metro, Basil Street, SW3 (see p. 55); Harrods, Knightsbridge; Bendick's and GTC, Sloane Street, SW3; Ménage à Trois, Beauchamp Place, SW3; La Tante Claire, 68 Royal Hospital Road, SW3; Walton's, 121 Walton Street, SW3. **Local shopping** Harrods and other Knightsbridge stores; Sloane Street and King's Road boutiques. **Local interest** Natural History, Science, Geological, and Victoria & Albert Museums; Royal Albert Hall; Hyde Park and Kensington Gardens.

A floating Victorian hotel

In 1875 Captain Webb became the first man officially recorded as swimming the English Channel unaided. He made many other record-setting swims along the Thames, which is why Paul and Gaynor Waterman felt it appropriate to name their 1890s Dutch-built barge after him.

This unique floating Victorian hotel has solid mahogany woodwork and is furnished with elegant bric-à-brac, comfortable settees, potted plants, and cane-seated chairs under a quilted silk ceiling. The open deck area, with flowering shrubs in pots, provides further space to laze about. The cabin bedrooms are modern, with excellent showers, constant hot water, ingenious and immaculate private facilities, flowered wallpaper, and fitted white furniture, including chests of drawers and hanging closets. Any extra baggage can be safely stowed aboard elsewhere. Firm, full-sized mattresses and cosy duvets ensure sound sleep.

You can wake to Windsor Castle glimpsed through the morning mist, framed in willow trees, take afternoon tea while snow-white swans drift slowly past in leafy Richmond, or watch the sun set over Greenwich Palace and the masts of teaclipper *Cutty Sark*. The boat moors at the foot of the Tower of London, and beside Hampton Court palace, where you can have an elegant private picnic in the Queen's Privy Garden, by special permission.

The atmosphere on board is more that of a house party than of a hotel. The twelve guests and six crew members are all introduced by Christian names only. There is an exciting feeling of all setting out on an expedition together, except that you sit back and are pampered, lingering over breakfast with the morning's papers, or chatting on the radio telephone while the crew neatly maneuver the boat through amazingly engineered locks or prepare meals from fresh ingredients in the spotless modern galley.

Dinner on board, at a long table elegantly set and adorned with candles and fresh flowers, may include crab and asparagus mousse, Charles II's favorite fresh salmon in champagne with dill, and sweet nuts and peaches, a dish created to tempt the palate of Mary Tudor. The recipes were discovered by Gaynor in the libraries of the Thames-side palaces.

The Waterman's two young sons and two dogs are also aboard, but discreetly invisible, appearing occasionally to walk the towpath. Companies or groups of friends can charter their own private cruises in *Captain Webb*, Gaynor however reserving control of the menus. Those who enjoy boats, rivers, good food, and exploration will find life aboard *Captain Webb* both relaxing and fun.

Opposite: two views of the surprisingly spacious main cabin and a prospect of the Thames from the deck; Tower Bridge looms in the background. One of the boat's two friendly dogs is shown above. Overleaf: the full extent of the barge is revealed as it passes the Tower of London.

CAPTAIN WEBB, c/o Another Britain, White Cross, Water Lane, Richmond, Surrey. **Tel.** On board: (0836) 202408. **Telex** No. **Owners** Another Britain Co. **Managers** Paul and Gaynor Waterman. **Open** All year. **Rooms** 2 single, 2 double, 3 twin, all with private bathroom (no tubs, showers only), airconditioning and central heating. **Facilities** Cruises as arranged, available moored for dinner parties. Boat is 105 ft. long and 19 ft. 8½ in. wide. Open sundeck, sitting room, dining room areas, closecarpeted, with airconditioning and central heating, radio telephone, laundry by arrangement, bar, small library, complimentary morning papers. **Restrictions** None. **Terms** Expensive, but all meals and a champagne welcome, sherry, châteaux-bottled wines, buffet luncheons, afternoon tea, and morning coffee are included. **Credit cards** Visa/Diners Club, but personal checks preferred. **Distance from transport** The ship moors beside places to be visited. Any more distant sightseeing is by complimentary taxi or small private coach. Arrangements are made to collect or deliver passengers from or to airport or hotel. **Local shopping/Local interest** A complimentary visit to the theater is generally included, and help and advice with ongoing shopping and touring is very expertly supplied. The highlights of the usual tour include Greenwich, Southwark Cathedral, the Tower of London, Hampton Court, and Windsor. There are also special interest trips; enquire when booking.

Claridge's

Magnificence revived

As in the story of the emperor who had no clothes, for the past few years nobody presumed to stand up and complain publicly about the growing shabbiness of Claridge's. How could anybody criticize what was virtually an annex of Buckingham Palace, praised by Queen Victoria in the 1850s, home from home for visiting kings, art deco gem of the 1930s with a tradition going back to 1812? Happily, England's most prestigious hotel has recently undergone a miraculous transformation under its new General Manager, Ronald Jones.

Nothing, heaven forbid, has been radically altered. But the liveried retainers, though stately and dignified as ever, have become once again attentive and concerned. The black-and-white marble floors shine, walls have been redecorated, carpets renewed, and the elaborately intertwined bronze heraldic shields gleam on the main staircase's sweeping balustrade. Air-conditioning has been unobtrusively installed in the famous restaurant, and in most of the bedrooms. The traditional mixture of priceless antiques, comfortable chairs, fine china, prints, elegantly carved fireplaces, statuary, and oil paintings remains unchanged, but spruced up. Those guests requiring their clothes to be unpacked, brushed and pressed, and their baths drawn to a specific temperature may have these services as impeccably performed as they would have been 170 years ago under the auspices of M. Mivert, French chef and first owner of the premises, or subsequently under Mr Claridge, former butler to the nobility.

When I arrived late one morning, ravenous, having left an unpleasant hotel after an uncomfortable night without stopping to eat, breakfast was upon request instantly wheeled in to my room. It was arranged on a starched gray linen cloth, and the delicious coffee was served in huge green and gold Wedgwood china cups decorated with a coronetted "C." The orange-juice was freshly squeezed, the croissants warm, and all, smilingly, at noon. My room, decorated with pretty sprigged paper, had enormous mirror-fronted hanging closets with towelling robes inside, a charming antique desk with dip-pen and inkwell, a color television, a supremely comfortable bed, and softest of down pillows. The fine linen sheets were changed when rumpled by my afternoon nap. An archway led to a gray marble bathroom with accessories beautifully set out on a white linen cloth, a huge bathsheet warming on a hot rail, and an excellent shower.

Dinner was highly enjoyable. Tempting *hors d'oeuvres* were followed by salmon trout with a sharp sorrel sauce, creamed spinach, and tiny new potatoes. Wild strawberries, coffee, and petits-fours completed an elegantly and courteously served meal. Ronald Jones has great pride in this historic building and his trust and confidence in his staff have inspired them. This is a newly impressive Claridge's.

Opposite: Champagne and exotic fruit wait beside the bed of a fortunate guest. Above is a gleaming art deco interior; more 1930s splendor is shown overleaf (left). D'Oyly Carte's piano is preserved in the Royal Suite (right, top). The hotel's traditional English breakfast provides a hearty start to the day.

CLARIDGE'S, Brook Street, W1A 2JQ. **Map reference** 21. **Tel.** (01) 629 8860. **Telex** 21872. **Owners** The Savoy Hotel plc. **General Manager** Ronald Jones. **Open** All year. **Rooms** 61 single, 89 double, 52 suites, 3 royal suites, all with bathroom (including shower), color TV, direct-dial phone, radio. **Facilities** Restaurant, reading room, elevator, The Causerie (smorgasbord restaurant at lunchtime: *à la carte* dinner), hairdresser, barber, flower shop, antique shop, 24-hr. maid/waiter/valet service, Hungarian Orchestra, safe. **Restrictions** No dogs. **Terms** Expensive. **Lunch/Dinner** (in restaurant) Expensive.

Credit cards All major cards. **Nearest tube station** Bond Street, 200 yds. **Hotel parking** No. NCP in Cavendish Square, W1. **Local eating** Justin de Blank, 54 Duke Street, W1 (snacks); The Connaught (see p. 37); Scott's, 20–22 Mount Street, W1. **Local shopping** Bond Street; Cork Street commercial art galleries; young designer fashions in South Moulton Street; Regent Street stores (Laura Ashley, Jaeger, Liberty's); Burlington Arcade; Savile Row bespoke tailors and men's wear. **Local interest** Wallace Collection (art treasures); Wigmore Hall (concerts); Royal Academy; Museum of Mankind.

The Connaught

Exclusive grandeur

The Connaught remains unchangingly superb over the years. This exclusive hotel, just off Grosvenor Square and only a few steps away from the American Embassy, has a smartly uniformed doorman, instantly alert porters, and formal but welcoming desk staff. A series of elegant and comfortable but not overwhelming public rooms leads from the small central hall. Service is swift, attentive, and expert, and I had the impression of being the guest in some charming small palace or distinguished private residence rather than in a hotel. A solid oak staircase – or leisurely, period elevator – leads up to wide corridors, hung with huge oil paintings. Each bedroom has its own foyer, antique furniture, and splendid bathroom.

The food is magnificent and is served with great style. I thought it appropriate to invite to luncheon my husband's aunt, a grande dame, once lady-in-waiting to a now long-vanished royal court, and she pronounced The Connaught a survival of all that had been best in the luxury hotels she had known throughout Europe in the 1930s. Together we enjoyed quail eggs, served on an artichoke-based cream in a shell of meltingly light pastry, a dish of scallops, lobster, shrimps, and sole presented together in a perfectly seasoned sauce, followed by featherlight fresh strawberry mille-feuilles and delicious coffee. Dishes were presented for approval before being served, stiffly starched white tablecloths were changed by expert sleight of hand between courses without removing anything from the table, and the entire meal was of a quality that made me astonished Michelin should have deprived the hotel of one of the two stars it originally awarded. At night my bed was turned down, my nightclothes were laid out, and a small white linen mat was placed beside the bed, so that my bare feet would not encounter the carpet, a courtesy once current but now rare. In the morning, I had only to touch one of the bedside bells for a smiling waitress to come to my door. She wrote down my breakfast requirements and reappeared five minutes later with a well-laden, linen-covered trolley. The valet, similarly summoned, bore away my suit for pressing and a maid went hurrying off to find a housekeeper, who instantly produced a hairdryer at my request.

Since The Connaught maintained its standards throughout a time when other hotels of similar character – now newly restored – were in decline, it has acquired a fiercely loyal clientèle who refuse to stay elsewhere. As a result it has become almost a private club, and guests book next year's visit during this year's and commend their friends to the manager. Should you wish to stay or have a meal here you must book very far ahead, and even then be prepared for disappointment.

Opposite and above: the imposing portico and stately façade on Carlos Place of this most aristocratically exclusive of hotels.

THE CONNAUGHT, Carlos Place, W1Y 6AL. **Map reference** 18. **Tel.** (01) 499 7070. **Telex** 296376. **Owners** The Savoy Hotel plc. **Managing Director and General Manager** Paolo Zago. **Open** All year. **Rooms** 90 rooms, all with bathroom (including shower), color TV, direct-dial phone. **Facilities** 24-hr. room service, sitting room, drawing room, restaurant, bar, Grill Room, elevator, safe. **Restrictions** None. **Terms** Expensive. **Lunch/Dinner** Expensive. **Credit cards** All major cards. **Nearest tube station** Bond Street, $\frac{1}{4}$ mile. **Hotel parking** No. NCP in Cavendish Square, W1. **Local eating** Claridge's (see p. 33); Scott's, 20–22 Mount Street, W1; The Dorchester (see p. 39); The Greenhouse, 27a Hay's Mews, W1. **Local shopping** Bond Street; Burlington Arcade. **Local interest** American Embassy and Roosevelt Memorial, Grosvenor Square; Royal Academy; Museum of Mankind.

The Dorchester

Park Lane perfection

The Dorchester bakes its own bread twice daily. In the Spanish-style, tapestry-hung Grill Room guests are offered not a small selection of rolls, but a marvellous assortment of loaves – woven, plaited, baked in a flower-pot, milk bread, wholemeal, with or without poppy or sesame seeds. It is not surprising that even such a detail as the quality of the bread should be so outstanding, since by popular consensus The Dorchester has in Anton Mosimann the finest chef in London. Mr Mosimann has pioneered *Cuisine Naturelle*, which uses only the freshest of fresh ingredients, simply cooked, without oil, butter, cream, or wine, although his repertoire also includes elaborate classic French dishes. Dinner in the Terrace Restaurant is something to remember, beautifully served amid the pretty Chinese-inspired décor. Beef consommé with beef marrow dumplings, fillets of sole with a light ginger and tomato sauce, stuffed guinea fowl with braised chicory and wild mushrooms, lemon and pear liqueur parfait with fresh raspberry purée, coffee and delicate *delices des dames* sweetmeats were all superb.

Sometimes described as looking like a luxury liner moored beside green Hyde Park, The Dorchester has been magnificently restored to its original 1930s glory. The Promenade is astonishing: as I entered the elegant balconied hall hung with vast crystal lanterns, and caught sight of the formal marbled, gilded, and pillared vista ahead, I thought its apparent size was achieved by mirrors, but walking down its 165-feet length I found it to be no illusion. It is a most agreeable place to take afternoon tea: delicious sandwiches, pastries, and a selection of fine teas are swiftly and attentively served.

Bedrooms in The Dorchester are comfortable and spacious, some with 1930s tubs still intact in the bathrooms and some with airconditioning. Beds have linen sheets and the room-service menu is excellent. There are large corner suites, and opulent deluxe Roof Garden suites with balconies and flower-filled windowboxes. The Penthouse has a magnificent reception suite, with painted ante-rooms, a mirrored dining room, and a balcony overlooking London, on which is a goldfish pool backed by a statue of Leda and the Swan. This must be the most spectacular place in London in which to entertain. Tucked away out of sight downstairs are two splendid blue ballrooms with elaborate reception rooms and private entrances on Park Lane and Deanery Street. The mirrored bar is charmingly decorated with blue and white ceramic tiles handpainted with fantastic birds in ornate cages.

The hotel has changed hands several times in recent years. It is to be hoped that its current magnificence will be maintained with pride by its new owner, the Sultan of Brunei.

Opposite: the vast length of the magnificent Promenade is lined by gilded statuettes. The Dorchester's food is thought by many to be the finest in London. This exquisitely arranged dish of scallops in saffron sauce is garnished with tomato and dill. A statue of Leda and the Swan decorates the fishpond in the Penthouse suite (above). Overleaf is the glittering bar.

THE DORCHESTER, Park Lane, W1A 2HJ. **Map reference** 16. **Tel.** (01) 629 8888. **Telex** 887704. **Owner** The Sultan of Brunei. **General Manager** Wolfgang Nitschke. **Open** All year. **Rooms** 80 single, 136 double, 67 suites, 5 luxury suites, all with bathroom (including shower), color TV, radio, mini-bar. **Facilities** 24-hr. room service, elevators, baby sitting, flower shop, hairdressing and beauty salon, in-house doctor, bookstall, restaurant, grill room, bar, library, 2 ballrooms, 6 further reception rooms, penthouse private dining and reception rooms, Promenade, safes, shoeshining, same-day laundry/drycleaning/valeting service (weekdays only). **Terms** Expensive. **Lunch/Dinner** Expensive. Expensive fixed-price lunch and dinner menus. **Credit cards** All major cards. **Nearest tube station** Hyde Park Corner, 500 yds. **Hotel parking** Yes, for *c*.50 cars. **Local eating** The Greenhouse, 27a Hay's Mews, W1; Scott's, 20–22 Mount Street, W1; Mirabelle, 56 Curzon Street, SW1; The Connaught (see p. 37); The Athenaeum Hotel (see p. 11). **Local shopping** Harrods and other Knightsbridge stores; Bond Street; Piccadilly; Burlington Arcade; Oxford Street. **Local interest** Hyde Park and Kensington Gardens; Apsley House (Wellington Museum); Wallace Collection.

Dukes Hotel

St James's

A well-kept secret

The quality of Dukes Hotel can best be described as quiet excellence. More than at any other London hotel, to arrive at this privately owned, exclusive, and elegant establishment gives the impression of coming home to one's own very grand and very well-run mansion. Perhaps this is because it is in a tiny cul-de-sac off an already quiet street leading from St James's and has its own private courtyard, full of flowers and still gas-lit at night. Perhaps it is because of the lack of fuss about all the services provided. The 38 bedrooms and 14 suites are simple, but handsome and scrupulously maintained and great snowy heaps of huge white bathsheets are kept warm on hot rails in the impeccable modern bathrooms. The only word of complaint I have heard in many years of knowing Dukes was about the bedrooms' generally modest size, but now even this has been rectified by enlarging those on the upper floor.

The reception rooms, with patterned plaster ceilings, have kept their charmingly Edwardian character. It takes only a glance and a quiet word instantly to produce a drink, a tray of teatime goodies, or a mouth-watering menu as you sit in the small panelled bar, furnished with leather chairs and hung with ducal portraits, or in the cosy little drawing room, or in the tiny alcoved dining room, decorated with *trompe l'oeil* paintings. By some magic, I have never found any of the public rooms, or indeed the hallway, uncomfortably crowded, although one would expect incoming and outgoing visitors and their suitcases to meet at some point.

When eating in the restaurant, I was just beginning on a delicious terrine of lobster and smoked salmon, with accompanying tarragon-flavored lobster sauce,

when the kitchen sent out some slices of freshly baked warm brioche which they rightly suggested would with its slight sweetness enhance the lobster. Rosily pink lamb fillet in a light herb sauce and fresh vegetables melted in the mouth, and Dukes' famous bread-and-butter pudding was even better than my mother used to make. Handmade petits-fours accompanied the excellent coffee.

A house has stood here since Charles II's time, but was rebuilt in 1895 as chambers for the sons of the nobility. Although it became a hotel in 1908, Dukes has never lost the atmosphere of a private residence, from which one may stroll across to the ancient little St James's shops to be measured for hand-made shirts, shoes, or hats, or go down to the flowery gardens of St James's Park. As the hotel likes to say, Dukes is one of London's best-kept secrets.

Opposite: a corner of one of the delightful bedrooms (top) and the panelled bar. The food (above) is especially notable.

DUKES HOTEL, 35 St James's Place, SW1A 1NY. **Map reference** 27. **Tel.** (01) 491 4840. **Telex** 28283. **Owner** Dukes Hotel Ltd. **Managing Director** Richard Davis. **Open** All year. **Rooms** 8 single, 28 double, 16 suites, all with bathroom (including shower), direct-dial phone, TV, radio. **Facilities** Drawing room, bar, dining room, elevator, 1 small and 1 large function room, secretarial service, same-day laundry/drycleaning/valeting/pressing service, 24-hr. room service, safe. **Restrictions** Not suitable for children under 8; no dogs. **Terms** Medium. **Lunch/Dinner** Medium. **Credit cards** All major cards. **Nearest tube station** Green Park, ¼ mile. **Hotel parking** No. NCP in Arlington Street, SW1. **Local eating** Fortnum and Mason's and the Royal Academy, both in Piccadilly, for light meals; Green's Champagne and Oyster Bar, 35–36 Duke Street, SW1; Suntory, 72 St James's Street, SW1; Le Caprice, Arlington House, Arlington Street, SW1; Wilton's, 55 Jermyn Street, SW1; Mirabelle, 56 Curzon Street, SW1; The Ritz (see p. 77); The Stafford (see p. 87). **Local shopping** Jermyn Street for menswear, and English perfume at Floris; Burlington Arcade; Fortnum and Mason's, Simpson's, Hatchard's (books), Piccadilly; Burberry's, Haymarket. **Local interest** Royal Academy; Museum of Mankind; Design Centre, Haymarket; National Gallery and National Portrait Gallery; St James's Park, Green Park, and Buckingham Palace.

Ebury Court

Belgravia

Civilized simplicity

It is highly unusual to come upon a London hotel that has been under the same owner-management for 45 years, but then Ebury Court is not a usual hotel. It belongs to Diana Topham, once a pupil at Cheltenham Ladies' College, and her husband, Romer, formerly a barrister of Lincoln's Inn. Since it is a home – their daughter was raised here and other members of the family have helped out in times of crisis – it has a specially domestic and very British atmosphere that is much appreciated by country gentry and visiting anglophiles alike. The same guests have returned so often that they have their own private clubroom and bar; drinks are brought to other visitors upon request.

The hotel occupies a graceful row of five small houses that was being built while Queen Victoria and Prince Albert were raising their large family half-a-mile away in Buckingham Palace. The mood is civilized, fairly formal, but warm and welcoming. A restaurant with cozy alcoves and low ceilings has been created in what were once cellars and store rooms. The food is the best sort of traditional home cooking, with sausages from the Queen's supplier, bread baked every day to a recipe given to Mrs Topham by a nun, and beef from Scotland. The 39 delightful small color-washed bedrooms are not for those travelling with large amounts of heavy luggage, or seeking self-indulgent luxury. Much of the furniture is plain, and painted white; the hanging closets are tiny, but the chests of drawers provide useful extra space. Bathrooms are *en suite* wherever the mid-1800s architecture allows; where it does not, they are a short walk down the corridor. Some have showers. Possessions accumulated over the years include the family Hepplewhite four-poster; a wing chair and grandfather clock which belonged to Romer's father, Judge Topham; a genuine featherbed that needs the porter's help to turn; porcelain hand-painted door

knobs; and some good antiques. Bedlinen is crisp and there are lovely chintzes.

Arriving hot and exhausted for lunch, unbooked, at the height of the tourist season, and at nearly two in the afternoon, I was warmly welcomed and a seat was found for me in the restaurant. I was made to feel special though I had never set foot there before, and this impression was reinforced when I returned to stay. Ebury Court is not designer decorated, but has the comfortably lived-in and loved feeling of the family house that it is. Winner of the prestigious César Award from the *Good Hotel Guide* for "maintaining old-fashioned hotel virtues in the metropolis," it embodies – like its kindly, unobtrusive, and gracious owners – all that is best in Britain.

The prettily draped four-poster bed opposite and attractive antique writing desk above are typical of the old-world charm of this friendly hotel.

EBURY COURT, 26 Ebury Street, SW1 W0LU. **Map reference** 6. **Tel.** (01) 730 8147. **Telex** No. **Owners** Romer and Diana Topham. **Open** All year. **Rooms** 21 single and 18 double, of which 12 have bathrooms (some with showers); all have radio and phone. Color TV can be hired. **Facilities** Elevator, sitting room, writing room (with TV), club bar, restaurant, safe, pre-theater suppers available from 6.30 pm. **Restrictions** No children under 5 in restaurant; small well-behaved dogs only. **Terms** Moderate (English breakfast included). **Lunch/Dinner** Moderate. **Credit cards** Access/Visa. **Nearest tube station** Victoria, 100 yds. (NB Victoria rail station provides direct link to Gatwick Airport.) **Hotel parking** No. NCP in Semley Place, SW1. **Local eating** Ciboure, 21 Eccleston Street, SW1; The Goring Hotel (see p. 51); The Berkeley (see p. 15). Memories of China, 67–69 Ebury Street, SW1. **Local shopping** Army and Navy Stores, Victoria Street. **Local interest** Buckingham Palace (Royal Mews and Queen's Gallery are open to the public); St James's Park; Green Park; Westminster (RC) Cathedral.

Orchids and champagne

It is fitting that Fortyseven Park Street should choose an orchid as its symbol. The marble entrance hall of this luxurious establishment leads, by elevator or graceful curving staircase, to 54 Edwardian-style high-ceilinged suites, built in the 1920s. Continental elegance has been combined with transatlantic understanding. Your morning coffee and croissants, or eggs and bacon, are brought to you by a staff with charming French accents; Continental white-linen-covered, down-filled duvets are on the beds; champagne – Joseph Perrier cuvée royale as supplied to Queen Victoria – and a vase of delicate orchids await your arrival, courtesy of the management. Each peaceful, doubleglazed and airconditioned suite has a gleaming marble bathroom with soft Christy towels and robes, and an efficient shower; those on the top floor have antique furniture. Bedrooms are un-cluttered, with good mirrors and well-placed light-ing, and ample hanging space for clothes. There are push-button direct-dial phones in both bedroom and sitting room, comprehensive mini-bars, large remote-controlled color televisions, and a tiny, well equipped all-electric galley kitchen, which will be fully stocked on request.

Fortyseven Park Street has no restaurant of its own, but it adjoins Le Gavroche, London's only Michelin three-star restaurant, from where appetiz-ing light snacks and salads, or more lavish meals by prior arrangement, can be sent up to your room directly. Should you wish to eat in the restaurant, it is as well to make your reservation when booking your room, since tables are always very much in demand. A private door leads from the hotel into Le Gavroche. Meals here are an event. The low-ceilinged, dark-green dining room gleams in the candlelight with polished silver and shining glassware, and has a profusion of beautifully arranged fresh flowers. The

service is impeccable. The wine list, which contains only the best vintages of the best wines, is a connoisseur's delight and the menu, in French only, is adventurous and creative. I found the soufflé suissesse, a light cheese soufflé daringly flipped over while cooking, and served with a creamy sauce, delicious, though I query serving madeira sauce with the otherwise delectable seabass and salmon-trout. Perfect apricot icecream, a large dish of freshly made petits-fours, and excellent coffee completed the meal.

Fortyseven Park Street is run by manager Keith Bradford with polished expertise and charm. Just off Park Lane, in the heart of Mayfair, and only a short distance from the American Embassy, it is an ideal base for several days in London's most exclusive residential area.

Opposite is the main staircase, with splendid stained glass; above is a marble bathroom. Overleaf: left, champagne for two in an apartment and the famed restaurant Le Gavroche, which adjoins the hotel; right, a charming pastel-painted bedroom.

FORTYSEVEN PARK STREET, 47 Park Street, W1Y 3HD. **Map reference** 19. **Tel.** (01) 491 7282 (Le Gavroche: (01) 408 0881). **Telex** 22116. **Owners** Fortyseven Park Street Ltd. **General Manager** Keith Bradford. **Open** All year. **Rooms** 54 twin-bedded suites, with 1 or 2 bedrooms, sitting room, bathroom (including shower), and kitchen. All have direct-dial phones and color TV; some have optional airconditioning and own safe. **Facilities** Elevator, room service, 24-hr. reception, maid service, key-card security, same-day laundry/dry cleaning service, secretarial service, theater bookings, safe. **Restrictions** Bookings must be for at least 3 days. **Terms** Expensive. **Lunch/Dinner** (in Le Gavroche) Expensive. **Credit cards** All major cards. **Nearest tube station** Marble Arch, ¼ mile. **Hotel parking** No. NCP in Park Lane, W1, or parking in Selfridge Hotel, Orchard Street, W1. **Local eating** The Dorchester (see p. 39); The Connaught (see p. 37); Scott's, 20–22 Mount Street, W1; **Local shopping** Bond Street; Burlington Arcade; Piccadilly stores; Cork Street commercial art galleries. **Local interest** Wallace Collection; Royal Academy; Museum of Mankind; Wig-more Hall; Hyde Park.

The Goring Hotel

Beside Buckingham Palace

Should you wish to call officially upon the Queen, or attend a royal garden party, you will find The Goring very convenient. It is in a quiet side street beside Buckingham Palace, just round the corner from the Royal Mews, so that the carriage sent for distinguished visitors can wait in front of the hotel's front door without holding up the traffic and will then have only a gentle half-mile for the horses to trot to reach the palace's main gates. When any large official occasion is in progress the hotel is always in demand as an honorary extra wing to the palace. This is a role it fulfils with distinction, for it is a handsome Edwardian building, immaculately kept, the outside decorated with flowering windowboxes. The stately entrance hall has a black-and-white marble floor, pale-blue and white décor, and deep blue carpets. Beyond is a spacious and comfortable lounge and bar which look into a central garden whose neatly trimmed lawns and tidy flowerbeds cover an area once crammed with notorious slum houses.

The first Mr Goring built his hotel in 1910 in what was then an unfashionable area, foreseeing the demand there would be for accommodation for passengers to the Continent setting off from nearby Victoria Station, then approaching completion. It is still a family hotel, run by the grandson of the founder. Many of the staff have served succeeding generations, and, like family retainers, are extremely concerned about the comfort and care of the guests.

In the welcoming restaurant, dishes are not served ready arranged in modest portions as in *nouvelle cuisine*. Waiters solicitously ply you with generous helpings of roast meats, delicious fresh vegetables, and succulent desserts. The bedrooms, many recently redecorated, are either wood panelled and traditional, or fresh and chintzy. Mine had a brass bedstead, pretty peach-pink easy chairs, a desk, and a substantial range of Edwardian fitted cupboards.

There was a large modern bathroom with dark blue tiles, an excellent shower, and plenty of towels.

The hotel's history is well documented in a book by the first Mr Goring's son, which can be purchased here. It is not only monarchs and their entourages who appreciate the old-world courtesy and traditional comforts of the hotel. Any of its guests will tell you that "they really look after you at The Goring."

Portraits of the Goring family and photographs of their staff are proudly displayed in their hotel (above). Opposite is a pretty chintzy bedroom. Overleaf: left, a stairway topped by a flamingo; right, a view of the grassy square on to which the hotel backs, and one of the colorful windowboxes that brightens the façade.

THE GORING HOTEL, 15 Beeston Place, Grosvenor Gardens, SW1W 0JW. **Map reference** 7. **Tel.** (01) 834 8211. **Telex** 919166. **Owner** George Goring. **General Manager** William Cowpe. **Open** All year. **Rooms** 40 single, 45 double, 5 suites, all with bathroom (including shower), color TV, radio, direct-dial phone. **Facilities** 24-hr. room service (sandwiches and beverages only from 10.30 p.m. to 7.30 a.m.), elevator, restaurants, sitting room, bar, 5 private dining rooms, safes, same-day laundry/dry cleaning/valeting/shoe cleaning and mending services.

Restrictions No dogs. **Terms** Moderate. **Lunch/Dinner** Medium. Moderate lunch and medium dinner fixed-price menus. **Credit cards** All major cards. **Nearest tube station** Victoria, 100 yds. **Hotel parking** Yes, in mews opposite by arrangement (capacity 12 cars). **Local eating** Ciboure, 21 Eccleston Street, SW1. **Local shopping** Army and Navy Stores, Victoria Street. **Local interest** Buckingham Palace; St James's Park; St James's Palace; Westminster (R.C.) Cathedral.

French Provincial chic

Step through the rather grand marble doorway of L'Hotel, and you seem to have entered some delightful French country hotel, or rural New England Inn. The hall is wide and full of light, there are green plants, sisal matting on the floor, a wooden dresser with a row of white china hens, cream-colored walls stencilled faintly with wild roses and sheaves of corn, and a handsome stripped-pine desk behind which sits one of the staff, waiting to greet you. Enchanting modern primitive paintings of sheep and cattle against a background of bright blue sky and emerald grass hang on the walls. A staircase with splendid oak bannisters leads up past hanging antique quilts to 12 rooms with red-baize-covered, brass-studded doors, and down – past enlargements of *premier cru* wine labels – into Le Metro, the wine bar in the cellar.

The bedrooms are simple, but extremely civilized. Each has a pine desk and chair, a free-standing pine wardrobe, a Windsor chair, and a brass bedstead with fine linen sheets. There are pretty tiles in the good modern bathrooms, which have a tub and hand-shower. Mrs David Levin has deliberately kept L'Hotel's furnishings simple, since those who want more elaborate décor as well as more pampering service have the alternative of The Capital Hotel next door, also owned by her husband (see p. 27). With the busy and independent in mind, there is no room service; you are given the key to the front door, and the staff leaves at 6.00 p.m. In emergency you can, of course, always call on The Capital.

A splendid breakfast is served downstairs in Le Metro, which is also open to non-residents. The staff are here early in the morning, bustling about in their long white aprons to bring you delicious coffee in huge green and gold cups, hot fresh croissants and crunchy rolls, with plenty of unsalted French butter and home-made preserves – all included in the price of the room. Bentwood chairs, tables with curly

wrought-iron legs, an attractive bar, posters, and original sketches and cartoons on the walls add to Le Metro's charm and there is a tiny courtyard at the back with climbing plants on a trellis. A well-selected range of excellent-value wines are available by the glass or by the bottle. The food is both delicious and reasonably priced. Jambon persillé, salade frisée, and a tarte aux fraises simply heaped with fresh strawberries were memorable.

L'Hotel came into being fairly recently when David Levin acquired the then rather rundown little turn-of-the-century hotel from its somewhat eccentric lady owner and removed layers of wallpaper and paint to show the fine wood beneath. L'Hotel is now spruce and immaculate, a perfect Knightsbridge pied-à-terre.

The bedroom above is typical of L'Hotel's delightfully simple interiors. Opposite: a corner of one of the bedrooms and a mouthwatering breakfast from Le Metro; the group of naive pictures of farm animals hangs in the foyer.

L'HOTEL, 28 Basil Street, SW3 1AT. **Map reference** 10. **Tel.** (01) 589 6286. **Telex** 919042. **Owner** David Levin. **Managers** Pamela Vincent and Andrew Whiteford. **Open** All year. **Rooms** 12 double, all with twin beds, bathroom (with tub and handshower), color TV, direct-dial phone. **Facilities** Le Metro wine bar in cellar, safe. **Restrictions** Dogs at discretion of management. **Terms** Moderate. **Lunch/Dinner** (in Le Metro) Moderate. **Credit cards** American Express. **Nearest tube station** Knightsbridge, 50 yds. **Hotel parking** No. NCP in Pavilion Road, SW1.

Local eating The Capital Hotel (see p. 27); Harrods, Knightsbridge, and Bendick's and GTC, Sloane Street, SW1, for light meals; Menage à Trois, Beauchamp Place, SW3; La Tante Claire, 68 Royal Hospital Road, SW3; Walton's, 121 Walton Street, SW3. **Local shopping** Harrods and other Knightsbridge stores; King's Road and Sloane Street boutiques. **Local interest** Hyde Park and Kensington Gardens; South Kensington museums; Royal Albert Hall.

Marble halls

Mounted Horseguards, breastplates gleaming, plumed helmets with chinstraps severely in place, horses burnished like polished metal, ride out from Knightsbridge Barracks past the Hyde Park Hotel several times a week. This imposing edifice was built in Victorian times as a set of elegantly furnished apartments for gentlemen. It became a hotel at the turn of the century, and in the 1920s Rudolph Valentino was a guest. In 1948 George VI and Queen Elizabeth celebrated their Silver Wedding here, but in the 1960s it fell into a decline, from which it has now been triumphantly rescued.

Everything about the Hyde Park Hotel is on a huge scale. A wide steep flight of white marble stairs leads up to more, now carpeted, stairs, and into a vast mirrored and pillared chandelier-hung foyer, its severe lines softened by immense arrangements of fresh flowers, trailing plants, and potted palms. The glorious Portuguese pink, Sicilian white, and Verdi dark green marbles of the foyer were uncovered in the course of restoration, after years beneath layers of dreary paint and wallpaper. Lofty archways lead through to a spacious sitting area, and on into the Park Room, which directly overlooks the green magnificence of Hyde Park. Here you can enjoy a leisurely English breakfast, buffet lunch, formally served afternoon tea, or candlelit dinner. Menus are based on traditional dishes, attention is paid to detail, the quality and rapidity of the service are both irreproachable, and there is an excellent selection of reasonably priced quality wines. There are further private reception rooms, a ballroom resplendent in peach décor and regilded with real gold leaf, a mirrored drawing room, the Park Suite, and the King Gustav Adolphus Suite, favored by the late king of Sweden. All have been magnificently restored and are hung with Edwardian chandeliers. The dark-oak-panelled Grill Room has low ceilings, heavily embossed plasterwork, and, like the bar, the atmosphere of a club.

The bedrooms do not overwhelm. Known still as apartments, they are spacious and pleasingly proportioned and are furnished mainly with antique furniture; some have marvellous views of the park. The original hanging closets are large, the bedrooms' foyers have helpful extra space, there is good room service, a discreetly concealed mini-bar, and ultramodern bathrooms with good showers. Overnight laundry, valeting, and drycleaning services are most helpful.

It is heartening to see the owners, Trusthouse Forte, whose hotels usually have far more modest pretensions, investing so many millions with such dazzling results.

A chandelier-hung staircase is shown opposite; above is one of the hotel's many views of leafy Hyde Park. Overleaf: left, an exceptionally elegant bedroom (top) and one of the suites; right, a private dining room (top) and the main staircase.

HYDE PARK HOTEL, 66 Knightsbridge, SW1 Y7LA. **Map reference** 13. **Tel.** (01) 235 2000. **Telex** 262057. **Owners** Trusthouse Forte. **General Manager** Aldo Grosso. **Open** All year. **Rooms** 16 single, 145 double, 19 suites, all with bathroom (including shower), direct-dial phone, color TV, mini-bar, airconditioning. **Facilities** Elevators, restaurant, grill room, reading room, bar, 24-hr. room service, laundry/drycleaning/valeting service (including overnight service), hairdresser, conference facilities, theater ticket desk, private box (safe). **Restrictions** No dogs in public rooms. **Terms** Medium. **Lunch/Dinner** Medium. Moderate fixed-price lunch menu. **Credit cards** All major cards. **Nearest tube station** Knightsbridge, beside hotel. **Hotel parking** No. Nearest is in large garage serving hotel, for which fee is charged. **Local eating** The Capital Hotel (see p. 27); Le Metro, Basil Street, SW3 (see p. 55); Menage à Trois, Beauchamp Place, SW3; Harrods; Bendick's and GTC, Sloane Street, SW1, for light snacks. **Local shopping** Harrods and other Knightsbridge stores, including Harvey Nichols and Scotch House; Sloane Street boutiques. **Local interest** Hyde Park and Kensington Gardens; South Kensington museums; Royal Albert Hall.

The May Fair Hotel

History and comfort combined

What many visitors to London most enjoy is the opportunity to see live professional theater, opera, or ballet. For guests staying in The May Fair Hotel, this means walking only a few steps into the Mayfair Theatre, which is actually inside the hotel, just beside the restaurant. When I was staying, a thriller, *The Business of Murder*, was said to be all set to rival *The Mousetrap* as a long-running favorite.

The smartly uniformed doorman greets you warmly as you arrive at The May Fair. The long low marble hall has a vast arrangement of fresh flowers and an enormous chandelier hanging over the graceful ornate staircase which curves up to an oval landing. There is a convenient cluster of comfortable chairs and small tables in front of the long service desk, which is manned by pleasant and efficient staff. At one end of the hall, beside the newsstand, is a panelled bar, and a rather grand version of a traditional coffee shop, with starched linen tan-colored cloths on the tables, and a formally dressed manager, though with friendly waitresses. Reassuringly for those in culture shock, the menu includes chef's salad, pastrami on rye, burgers, and banana splits, as well as Dover sole, steak and kidney pie, and Scottish salmon, a selection much appreciated by the widely international clientèle. On the other side of the foyer is a formal restaurant, The Chateaubriand, which is arranged as a series of small, attractive rooms. The wine list includes many top vintages and a good variety of half bottles; the menu features especially delicious roast meats.

The bedrooms, all of which will soon have airconditioning, are agreeably furnished in reproduction antiques, some in pale wood, some in dark, with pretty flowered bedcovers. The framed photographs on the walls are of English stars who have appeared in the theater; bathrooms throughout are marble and modern. There is a series of larger studio double rooms with six-feet-wide beds and extra space for those with great quantities of luggage. As well as two vast deluxe suites, there is a penthouse with private entrance – an advantage for the owners of famous faces. The hotel's own Silver Spur Rolls Royce, complete with champagne bar and telephone, will take you shopping, to the airport, to the races, or touring.

Although now owned by an international chain, the traditions and original quality of this stately hotel, opened in 1927 by George V, are being respected. The May Fair is, I hope, destined to a new, elegant lease of life.

Opposite: The Chateaubriand restaurant (top) and the exotic Maharajah suite; the photographs beside the bed shown above are of stars who have appeared in the hotel's theater.

THE MAY FAIR INTER-CONTINENTAL HOTEL, Stratton Street, W1A 2AN. **Map reference** 23. **Tel.** (01) 629 7777. **Telex** 262526. **Owners** Inter-Continental Hotels. **General Manager** Patrick Board. **Open** All year. **Rooms** 83 single, 160 double, 52 suites (some with jacuzzi), 2 deluxe suites, 1 penthouse, all with bathroom (including shower), mini-bar, direct-dial phone, airconditioning. **Facilities** Elevators, restaurant, bar, coffee shop, news kiosk, 24-hr. laundry/dry cleaning service, 1-hr. pressing service, theater, shoe cleaning, chauffeured Rolls-Royce available, ballroom, conference suites, cinema. **Restrictions** None.

Terms Medium. **Lunch/Dinner** Expensive. Medium fixed-price lunch and dinner menus. **Credit cards** All major cards. **Nearest tube station** Green Park, 50 yds. **Hotel parking** No. NCP in Carrington Street, W1 (Shepherd Market). **Local eating** The Ritz (see p. 77); The Athenaeum Hotel (see p. 11); The Greenhouse, 27a Hay's Mews, W1. **Local shopping** Bond Street; Piccadilly stores; Burlington Arcade; Jermyn Street; Cork Street commercial art galleries. **Local interest** Royal Academy; Museum of Mankind; Green Park and Buckingham Palace.

The Montcalm

A Georgian mansion reborn

This is a hotel for those who like their history on the outside of the building and their modern comforts within. It stands in a lovely curved Georgian street built in 1789 and originally intended to be one half of a circular terrace, but the other half somehow never got built. The original porticoed façade and the 18th-century iron railings remain, beautifully maintained. The exterior is brightened by neat trees in tubs and windowboxes full of flowers. A welcoming doorman in dark brown and gold livery stands on the gleaming marble steps.

Once inside you are in a modern interior. The décor in the open-plan reception area, restaurant, and glittering bar is in the same soothing dark brown as the doorman's livery. Groups of extremely comfortable leather easy chairs and settees are scattered about, interspersed with large leafy plants in wooden pots, beautiful flower arrangements, and elegant antique desks for signing in. The total effect is sophisticated, yet pleasingly restful.

The whole hotel is climate controlled, a welcome luxury in English weather, and the bedrooms are pleasantly proportioned, without the claustrophobically low ceilings of many modern hotels. My single room had a queen-sized bed and military-campaign-style furniture, concealed in which were a large color television and a mini-bar. There was plenty of well-lit hanging and shelved space for clothes. Café-au-lait colored sheets, pale green walls, an apple-green carpet, and prints with touches of sharp pink formed an agreeable color scheme. I appreciated the built-in hairdryer, immaculate modern bathroom with many small extras, and the thick towelling robe.

The bedrooms at the front of the hotel have the original tall windows, but instead of making tall thin rooms the architect responsible for the conversion cleverly created delightful duplex suites. Each has a large comfortable sitting room, with ample space for entertaining, a fully-stocked bar, and an extra guest bathroom on the lower level. On the balcony above, reached by a charming wrought-iron spiral staircase, are the bed, hanging cupboards, and a larger bathroom. For the less spry there is a second entrance from the corridor at bedroom level.

The surrounding area has many pleasant Georgian houses and quiet squares, excellent chamber-music concerts in the Wigmore Hall, the world-famous Wallace Collection of armour, *objets d'art*, and paintings, and for shopping there is Selfridges practically on the doorstep. The Montcalm has recently been acquired by Japan Airlines, whose only changes will be the guiding influence of a master chef from their Paris hotel and an even more generous maintenance budget. Few hotels so successfully combine convenience and period charm.

Opposite: one of the antique reception desks; above: the Georgian portico and the hotel's doorman.

THE MONTCALM, Great Cumberland Place, W1A 2LF. **Map reference** 20. **Tel.** (01) 402 4288. **Telex** 28710. **Owners** Japan Airlines. **General Manager** Jonathan Orr Ewing. **Open** All year. **Rooms** 29 single, 74 double, 12 duplex suites, all with bathroom (including shower), color TV, direct-dial phone, radio, airconditioning, hairdryer. **Facilities** Restaurant, foyer sitting area, bar, elevator, 24-hr. room service, laundry/drycleaning/valeting/shoe mending services (same-day service on weekdays), baby sitting, safe.

Restrictions Small dogs only (on request and not in public areas). **Terms** Medium. **Lunch/Dinner** Medium. **Credit cards** All major cards. **Nearest tube station** Marble Arch, 50 yds. **Hotel parking** No. NCP in Great Cumberland Place, W1. **Local eating** The Connaught (see p. 37); Le Chef, 41 Connaught Street, W2; Genevive, 13 Thayer Street, W1. **Local shopping** Bond Street; Oxford Street. **Local interest** Wallace Collection; Wigmore Hall; Hyde Park.

52 Mount Park Road

A very English home

Elizabethan maps show "the waye from Uxbridge to London," which led through the market gardens of Ealing, past infamous Tyburn, site of public executions, to Oxford Street. A pleasant six-and-a-half mile drive from the city center, Ealing developed little until the arrival in Victorian times of the railway. Early photographs show hansom cabs waiting beside Haven Green in front of Ealing Broadway station, on the same cobblestones where taxicabs now stand.

At the far side of the Green, in a quiet leafy street in a conservation area, is the trim, rose-covered Victorian villa where the Curry-Townley-O'Hagans live. With the help of their two young sons they have transformed a once-neglected house with briar-patch garden into a gracious home. At the same time, Judith O'Hagan improved her knowledge of London history by taking a history degree, and her husband, Paddy, changed professions from stage and television actor to craft teacher at a local school, in order to spend more time with his family.

This is not a hotel as such; guests are welcomed as family friends, and reservations are essential. The bedrooms are comfortable, have duvets on the beds, and bathrooms with thermostatically controlled electric showers to outwit the eccentricities of Victorian plumbing. Lovely rugs embroidered by Judith's mother are scattered throughout the house, and among the many books on the shelves are several by her father, England's leading expert on donkeys. Judith's parents live on their own small Channel Island. Her grandfather, a peer, built and for many years was chairman of The Dorchester in Park Lane (see p. 39).

Judith is an expert cook, specializing in tempting traditional English breakfasts, which include honey from next door's bees. Dinner, if requested, is served by candlelight at the big polished table. Hot Stilton tartlets, turkey breast stuffed with herbs from the garden, home-made brandy-mousse icecream with sliced fresh strawberries and peaches were all excellent; the meal concluded with a selection of English cheeses, Judith's own handmade chocolate truffles, and delicious freshly ground coffee. Paddy O'Hagan, also with lordly antecedents – one cousin was page to the Queen – still sometimes appears on television, but he prefers entertaining his guests and working on the garden. The house is full of heirlooms gleaned from both sides of the family, enhanced by their own collection of pictures and prints. The O'Hagans are fascinating and thoughtful hosts, and their home provides a convenient base for trips to the stately houses and palaces that line the Thames, and to Oxford or Windsor, without the need to cross London.

Opposite: top, both inside and out, this quiet home has an air of welcoming tranquillity; bottom, pans gleam over the cooking range in the kitchen. Above: an antique lace fan makes an unusual decoration.

---

52 MOUNT PARK ROAD, W5 2RU. **Map reference** 31. **Tel.** (01) 997 2243. **Telex** No. **Owners** Paddy and Judith O'Hagan (NB affiliated Wolsey Lodge, In the English Manner, and At Home: see p. 7). **Open** All year, except 23 Dec.–2 Jan. **Rooms** 2 doubles, with bathroom including shower but not tub, further bathroom with tub. **Facilities** Sitting room, $\frac{3}{4}$-acre garden. **Restrictions** No dogs; no children under 6. **Terms** Moderate. **Lunch** No. **Dinner** On request only. Moderate (wine included). **Credit cards** No. Travellers checks, personal checks, or cash only.

Nearest tube station Ealing Broadway, $\frac{1}{4}$ mile. **Hotel parking** Yes. **Local eating** Small ethnic restaurants as recommended by hosts. **Local shopping** Large modern shopping mall. **Local interest** Gunnersbury Park (Rothschild mansion); Osterley Park and Syon Park (18th-cent. mansions); Ham House; Royal Botanical Gardens, Kew; Chiswick House; Marble Hill House; Hogarth's House; Heritage Motor Museum; Living Steam Museum; Musical Museum; Richmond Park; Hampton Court palace.

The New Piccadilly Hotel

Splendor restored

The New Piccadilly Hotel has been totally re-furbished. Close to Piccadilly Circus, it is within easy walking distance of many West End theaters and cinemas, Burberry's, Laura Ashley's, and Liberty's large stores, and the famous bespoke tailors of Jermyn Street. The interior is palatial. The vast magnificent Oak Room Restaurant has wood-panelled walls decorated with gilded trophies, garlanded leaves and flowers, helmets, swords, and shields in carved relief. Wonderful chandeliers, specially made in Italy, have wide swirling ribbons of glass and delicate crystal flowers glittering among the lights.

The former chef from Dukes Hotel (see p. 43) has been tempted over to run the kitchens, and he presides with sure, delicate touch over the *nouvelle-cuisine*-inspired dishes. His "Menu Surprise" in the Oak Room Restaurant is at first sight dauntingly long but it consists only of modest-sized dishes. A complimentary mini-kebab of duck was followed by salmon terrine with sauce verte, watercress soup in a tiny cup, and lobster, shrimp, and sole in a piquant sauce. After mango sorbet to clear the palate, there was lamb lightly grilled, a choice of cheeses – all in perfect condition – and a selection of exquisite desserts, finishing with coffee and petits-fours. Each of the eight beautifully presented, delicious courses provided most memorable mouthfuls. There is also a comprehensive selection of *à la carte* dishes.

The modestly sized bedrooms are fairly plainly furnished with reproduction antiques but the marble bathrooms are lavish. Clothes hanging space is surprisingly limited, and has clothes hangers of the irritating sort that are fastened to the rail. Many millions have been spent on 40,000 square feet devoted to recreation and fitness in a vast complex beneath the hotel. This includes a 12-meter

swimming pool surrounded by statuary and lush plants, two solaria, saunas, a Turkish bath, glass-backed squash courts, a nautilus gym, and a billiard room, as well as the Club Brasserie, drawing room, nightclub, and library. All are open to guests and to a limited number of private club members. Some suites overlook the glassroofed, palm-filled tropical splendors of the Terrace Garden Restaurant. The Bell's Whisky group, which owned both The New Piccadilly and the famous Gleneagles Hotel in Scotland, has recently been bought by the Guinness group. Let us hope the high standards that have been set in the restoration of this stately Edwardian hotel are maintained.

Opposite: top, the imposing marble-floored entrance hall; bottom, a pool in the glamorous recreation complex beneath the hotel. The splendid chandelier above is one of many throughout the hotel.

THE NEW PICCADILLY HOTEL, Piccadilly, W1V 0BH. **Map reference** 29. **Tel.** (01) 734 8000. **Telex** 25795. **Owners** The Guinness group. **General Manager** Patrick Fitz-gerald. **Open** All year. **Rooms** 110 single, 150 double, 30 suites, all with bathroom (including shower), color TV, radio, mini-bar. **Facilities** 24-hr. room service, 3 restaurants, lounge, safe, leisure complex (with billiards room, nightclub, squash courts, pool, sauna, jacuzzi, solarium, library, Turkish bath, nautilus gym), 24-hr. laundry/drycleaning service. **Restrictions** Dogs by request only. **Terms** Expensive. **Lunch** Brasserie/Terrace: Moderate; Oak Room: Medium (medium fixed-price menu also). **Dinner** Brasserie/Terrace: Moderate; Oak Room: Expensive. Expensive fixed-price "Menu Surprise" in Oak Room. **Credit cards** All major cards. **Nearest tube station** Piccadilly Circus, 50 yds. **Hotel parking** No. NCP in Brewer Street, W1. **Local eating** Inigo Jones, 14 Garrick Street, WC2; Gay Hussar, 2 Greek Street, W1; Poon's, 4 Leicester Street, W1, and many ethnic Soho restaurants. **Local shopping** Piccadilly and Haymarket stores; Burlington Arcade; Regent Street stores. **Local interest** Close to many theaters and cinemas. Trafalgar Square (National Gallery and National Portrait Gallery).

Number Sixteen

An art collector's delight

When I first set foot in Number Sixteen, I was not a guest. I arrived in Sumner Place exhausted, in a downpour on a hot day, with too much luggage, to stay in the hotel on the other side of the road, only to find that it was hidden by scaffolding. Bewildered by a series of unmarked doors with their doorbells disconnected, I struggled into Number Sixteen to throw myself on their mercy. They were sympathetic, welcoming, and amused, pointed out to me the correct entrance, and encouraged me to leave my suitcases with them until I had sorted out my problems. Returning later to stay, I therefore felt myself among friends.

Sumner Place is a perfect early Victorian street of graceful white-painted houses with pillared porticos. At one end there is bustling Old Brompton Road, with small useful shops, passing taxis, a post office, and an underground station with a direct link to both Heathrow and central London; at the other end is quiet, leafy Onslow Square.

Number Sixteen actually consists of four houses – numbers fourteen to seventeen. Their little back gardens are combined in a prize-winning, beautifully designed show of flowers, shrubs, and tall trees, all lovingly tended. The owner, Michael Watson, has greatly enjoyed restoring these delightful houses, now linked together on each floor by corridors which form galleries for the charming collection of pictures and prints he has acquired while hunting down exciting wallpapers, antique furniture, bathroom fittings, bibelots, and bedcovers. All the rooms are different sizes and shapes; showers, wash-hand basins, and often complete bathrooms have been fitted in as space allows. Each has its own name and décor. "The Navy Room," for instance, has navy-blue walls, a hand-painted wooden sign from The Armada pub in Portsmouth, prints of sailing ships, and nautical memorabilia. All but two rooms can be reached by elevator – mine, "Yellow," had a yellow waffle-pattern Welsh Weaver bedcover and hopeful pot of yellow begonias which harmonized with the furnishings, an agreeable mixture of antique and modern.

The hotel is staffed mainly by cheerful foreign students, as though by the offspring of a large friendly family. Only breakfast is provided, served in the bedrooms as there is no dining room, and kept deliberately simple in order that it can arrive exactly on time for those with appointments to keep. Every bedroom has a good list of recommended neighborhood restaurants, and there is an inhouse bar where guests help themselves and sign chits. Number Sixteen is an unpretentious but extremely civilized town-house alternative to London's more lavish hotels.

The graceful portico on Sumner Place (above) leads into elegantly furnished rooms filled with flowers and a choice collection of pictures. The disgruntled stone dwarf is a feature of the well-tended garden.

NUMBER SIXTEEN, 16 Sumner Place, SW7 3EG. **Map reference** 4. **Tel.** (01) 589 5232. **Telex** 266638. **Owner** Michael Watson. **Open** All year. **Rooms** 4 single, 28 double, some with bathroom (including shower), all with direct-dial phone, mini-bar, optional color TV. **Facilities** Elevator, garden, 3 sitting rooms, bar, safe, 24-hr. laundry/drycleaning service. **Restrictions** No dogs; no children under 12. **Terms** Moderate. **Lunch/Dinner** No. **Credit cards** All major cards. **Nearest tube station** South Kensington, 50 yds. **Hotel parking** No. NCP in Sloane Avenue, SW3. **Local eating** La Tante Claire, 68 Royal Hospital Road, SW3; St Quentin, 243 Brompton Road, SW3; Walton's, 121 Walton Street, SW3; The English Garden, 10 Lincoln Street, SW3; and see hotel's own guide. **Local shopping** Harrods and Knightsbridge stores; Walton Street boutiques. **Local interest** Natural History, Science, Geological, and Victoria & Albert museums; Royal Albert Hall; Hyde Park and Kensington Gardens.

An aristocratic apartment for antique-hunters

There are three flights of stairs to negotiate in order to reach this top-floor apartment, for there is no elevator. It is therefore commended mainly to the fit, who will find it well worth the climb.

Its owner, Mrs Sally Foster, though modestly disclaiming expertise as a professional interior designer, often works with friends who are, and has selected charming fabrics and wallpapers for her attractive and comfortable apartment, and for the pretty twin-bedded guest room. Tucked snugly under the eaves, this is reached by a further flight of internal stairs, and has a view through the stone balustrade over the trees in the gardens of the square. The adjoining bathroom has a shower, and is very well provided with accessories. Sally also puts a bottle of mineral water, chocolates, fruit, cookies, and books beside your bed.

Creator of designer knitwear and delicate patterns of fruit and flowers for embroidery specialists, painter, and professional restorer of fine porcelain, with a brother who sits in the House of Lords, Sally is also an inspired cook. If forewarned, she will provide newly-arrived guests with lunch or dinner. I was served a delicious cold soup of tomato, carrot, and red pepper, garnished with fresh chives, followed by fresh Scottish salmon with cucumber, hollandaise sauce, tiny shrimps, green salad, and garlic potatoes, finishing with orange icecream in a hot chocolate sauce sharpened with brandy. Sally, who is also a keen diner-out, will recommend her favorites among local restaurants.

The apartment is particularly well placed for antique-collectors as it is just round the corner from the Portobello Road and very near Kensington Church Street, two of London's best hunting grounds for expert and amateur antique-enthusiasts alike. Nearby is Kensington Palace, a royal residence;

the gardens and state apartments may be visited. The athletic will enjoy jogging through Kensington Gardens, the western extension of Hyde Park, enclosed by Henry VIII in the 16th century as hunting grounds. Children are traditionally taken there by their nannies to see the famous statue of Peter Pan, and to sail their toy boats on the large Round pond.

This is Sally's own home – her three children are sometimes here during school holidays – and those wishing to stay should contact In the English Manner, which organizes private visits to this and other equally appealing houses, including London mews cottages and stately homes in the country.

Opposite: the family sitting room, the snug bedroom, and a doll's house on the stairs; one of Sally Foster's cushions is shown above.

PEMBRIDGE SQUARE, W2. For booking, contact In the English Manner: see p. 7. **Map reference** 2. **Owner** The Hon. Mrs Sarah (Sally) Foster. **Room** 1 twin-bedded, with adjoining bathroom (including shower), color TV. **Facilities** Use of family sitting room, kitchen, and washing machine. **Restrictions** No dogs; no children under 5. **Terms** Moderate. **Lunch/Dinner** By arrangement only. Moderate. **Credit cards** No. Personal checks or cash only. **Nearest tube station** Bayswater or Queensway, 250 yds.

Hotel parking No. On-street parking usually available. **Local eating** Leith's, Monsieur Thompson's, and No 192, all in Kensington Park Road, W11; Julie's Restaurant and Bar, 137 Portland Road, W11; La Residence, 148 Holland Park Avenue, W11. **Local shopping** Portobello Road, Kensington Church Street (antiques). Street market in Portobello Road on Saturdays. **Local interest** Kensington Gardens, Kensington Palace.

Exuberant Victoriana

The Portobello is the brainchild of owner Tim Herring, manager Eva Lofstad, and designer Julie Hodges. It combines two delightful late Victorian terrace houses which back on to a quiet communal garden – a happy green wilderness of tall leafy trees and untidy but colorful flowerbeds. I arrived during a children's summer party, with a brass band playing and excited children in party clothes scampering about the grass among picnicking adults: all marvellously in period, but, happily for sleeping jet-lagged guests, a rare occurrence.

Tim Herring's friends, experienced international travellers with minimal luggage, were weary of callous and boringly stereotyped hotels with unwanted trappings. They yearned for somewhere with personality, informal, civilized, caring, and comfortable, with food available around the clock and friendly faces to greet them. Not finding anywhere exactly right, Tim Herring and his team have created such a haven.

The hotel is a fantasy on a Victorian military theme. There is mahogany campaign furniture in the bedrooms and throughout the houses are intriguing antiques, huge mirrors, potted plants, military prints, and twirly cast-iron bannister rails. The tiny elevator has a fierce grill door that snaps shut like a mousetrap, the ceilings have elaborate plaster coves, and the tall windows are curtained in Household Cavalry scarlet cloth. The light-filled, cheerful basement bar and restaurant, for hotel guests only, has 24-hour service of salads, snacks, hot dishes, coffee, sandwiches, and drinks. Everything is tasty, if fairly basic, and is served with friendly informality.

Bedrooms vary greatly in size and furnishings, but are priced accordingly. Minute single rooms are as compact as ships' cabins. My full-sized bunk-type bed had a snow-white, down-filled duvet, a color television suspended over it, a direct-dial telephone on the bulkhead, a folding-out reading light, canvas captain's chair, and compact storage and hanging space. There is a concealed mini-bar, a hot-water dispenser for the starter kit of tea and coffee, and croissants sealed in plastic, since there is no room service (full breakfast is served downstairs). All bathrooms are identical, lined in woven bamboo, with shower stall, mini wash-hand basin, and all other necessaries neatly stowed in ship-shape fashion. Double rooms have extra space and there are four exuberant suites – one with a round bed, draped with mosquito netting, and an amazing original free-standing bathtub, complete with many brass taps and complicated plumbing.

This is not a hotel for everyone, especially those much laden, but it is a wonderful find for independently-minded globe trotters, desperate for civilized takers of messages and guardians of mail and bored with fuss and flunkies.

Opposite: top, a tiny bedroom and the sitting room, its scarlet curtains reflected in an antique mirror; bottom, a table in the basement bar and restaurant. The hotel overlooks private gardens (above). Overleaf: left, one of the stylish suites; right, a view over trees from the hotel, and a four-poster bed.

PORTOBELLO HOTEL., 22 Stanley Gardens, W11 2NG. **Map reference** 1. **Tel.** (01) 727 2777. **Telex** 21879/25247 Attn: Portobello. **Owner** Tim Herring. **Manager** Eva Lofstad. **Open** All year, except one week at Christmas. **Rooms** 7 single, 11 double, 7 suites, all with bathroom (including shower but not tub), direct-dial phone, color TV. **Facilities** Elevator (to 3rd floor only), sitting room, safe, 24-hr. bar/restaurant. **Restrictions** None. **Terms** Moderate. **Lunch** Moderate. **Dinner** Medium. **Credit cards** All major cards. **Nearest tube station** Notting Hill Gate, $\frac{3}{4}$ mile. **Hotel parking** No. NCP in Queensway, W2. **Local eating** La Residence, 148 Holland Park Avenue, W11; Julie's Restaurant and Bar, 137 Portland Road, W11; The Ark, 35 Kensington High Street, W8. **Local shopping** Portobello Road and Kensington Church Street (antiques). Street market in Portobello Road on Saturdays. **Local interest** Architecture of Victorian crescents; Kensington Palace and Kensington Gardens; Holland Park. Neighborhood varies from very elegant to rather rough: ask hotel to identify appropriate areas.

The Ritz

A château in Piccadilly

The Ritz is a marvellous gilded Louis XVI château in the heart of London, planted on prim Piccadilly, overlooking Green Park, and fronted by its own Parisian-inspired arcade of elegant shops. César Ritz, the famed Swiss hotelier who guided The Savoy Hotel in its early days (see p. 83), caused two smaller hotels to be demolished to make way for England's first steel-framed building, which even in 1906 cost more than a million pounds.

Walk through the Piccadilly entrance and you will find yourself among a glittering array of mirrors, chandeliers, ornate plasterwork, flowers, dark-pink velvet-covered chairs and draperies. Facing you is the opulent Palm Court, with gilded statuary and an assembly of small tables, couches, and chairs, where even hotel guests must book well in advance if they wish to take the fabled afternoon tea. Running the length of the hotel, parallel with Piccadilly, is the high-ceilinged promenade of the Long Gallery, which leads to one of London's most elegant and ornate dining rooms. Gilded swags of foliage looped beneath a painted ceiling are reflected in long mirrors. Tall windows overlook a terrace decked with flower-filled urns, beyond which is a small garden. Dinner at night in this Cinderella's ballroom is by the light of pink candles set on tables spread with pink linen cloths and adorned with pink flowers; the food is served on pink and white Royal Doulton china. Former chef Michael Quinn is now at Ettington Park, near Stratford-upon-Avon; his replacement, David Miller, is a new rising star. Parma ham, freshly sliced, with melon ripe to perfection, lobster with a charmingly presented salad, papaya sorbet smooth as silk, and coffee from an ornate silver pot crowned with a silver pineapple, accompanied by petits-fours, were all delectable. The comprehensive wine list includes some exceptional clarets and armagnacs.

Next door is the private Marie Antoinette dining suite, a gilded and mirrored marvel.

My pale yellow and white painted bedroom had a huge antique mirror over an ornate marble mantelpiece, a yellow brocade cover on the extremely comfortable bed, big square down-filled pillows, and fine bedlinen laundered to perfect softness and embroidered with an "R." All the hotel bathrooms are super-modern, placing efficiency before nostalgia. A delicious breakfast in bed was served on a tray with pretty blue china.

The hotel sparkles and is full of life; the service is excellent, both efficient and concerned. Fully recovered from a 1960s slump, The Ritz is truly Ritzy once more.

Opposite: teatime in the luxurious Palm Court; above: the hotel from Green Park. Overleaf: left, a drawing room and an example of the superb cuisine – breast of corn-fed chicken filled with a double mousse of crayfish and chicken, resting on a light crayfish sauce, with white and spinach-flavored fine noodles. Right, a spectacular staircase.

THE RITZ, Piccadilly, W1V 9DG. **Map reference** 24. **Tel.** (01) 493 8181. **Telex** 267200. **Owners** Trafalgar House. **Managing Director** Michael Duffell. **Open** All year. **Rooms** 43 single, 81 double, 17 suites, all with bathroom (including shower), color TV, direct-dial phone, hairdryer; all with doubleglazing, some with airconditioning. **Facilities** 24-hr. room service, elevators, restaurant, Palm Court, Long Gallery, 3 private dining suites, ladies' and gentlemen's hairdresser, florist, kiosk, and theater desk. Same day laundry/drycleaning/valeting service. **Restrictions** No dogs (guide dogs excepted). **Terms** Expensive. **Lunch** Medium. Medium fixed-price menus. **Dinner** Expensive. Expensive fixed-price menu. **Credit cards** All major cards. **Nearest tube station** Green Park, 20 yds. **Hotel parking** No. NCP in Arlington Street, SW1. **Local eating** Fortnum and Mason's and Royal Academy, Piccadilly, for snacks; Green's Oyster and Champagne Bar, 35–36 Duke Street, SW1; Dukes Hotel (see p. 43). **Local shopping** Piccadilly stores; Burlington Arcade; Jermyn Street; Savile Row; Cork Street; Bond Street. **Local interest** Royal Academy; Museum of Mankind; Green Park and Buckingham Palace.

St James's Club

An art deco delight

Tucked away discreetly between The Ritz and St James's, the St James's Club is naturally as uncommunicative about its resident guests as any other leading London establishment. However it produces a magazine which reveals the identity of its titled, wealthy, and famous Honorary Committee assembled by owner Peter de Savary, and chronicles happenings in the club and in its sister establishment in Antigua. When passing through London this glitterati frequently elect to stay at the St James's Club where, sheltered from the curious and autograph seekers, they will find their friends and colleagues, and enjoy the exclusive and lavish comforts of the distinguished late Victorian building which has been sumptuously transformed by an inspired Italian design team.

The club's restrained opulence is a variation on the late 1920s art deco style that flourished in Hollywood at its peak. Meticulously maintained, highly professionally managed, it has a welcoming bar in earth tones and leather and a reposeful restaurant with olive-green velvet benches, carved wooden chairs with dusty-pink upholstered backs, and charming line drawings after Erté. The service is excellent and the menu is composed with a real understanding of the needs of the world traveller. As is common in America, but so rare alas in London, it provides what the jet-lagged might actually want to eat and drink, rather than what the chef dictates and the wine waiter suggests. You can be served, with equal deference and attention, a magnum of Chateau Latour '59, smoked salmon, and roast duckling, or a simple meal of sausages and mashed potatoes.

The suites have high ceilings and shimmer with reflected light from the many mirrors. My room was

in café-au-lait and blues, the bedspread forget-me-not blue faintly patterned with tiny butterflies, and the plump settee was covered in gentian-blue velvet. Ladies travelling alone find fresh flowers waiting in their room, which already has toning arrangements of silk flowers. Each suite, from studio to penthouse, is different in size and shape, but all have excellent showers, well-stocked bars, ample storage space, and orchid-colored monogrammed sheets and towels. Doubleglazing and airconditioning ensure undisturbed slumbers. Carved in marble over the bath is a scallop shell, emblem of St James, and worn in medieval times by pilgrims to his shrine at Santiago de Compostela.

After the initial visit, guests hoping to return must apply for membership. As with all prestigious clubs, one may have to wait to achieve that distinction.

Opposite: a beautifully designed bedroom and a corner of the bar; above, a snooker table in the billiard room – note the cartoons on the walls.

ST JAMES'S CLUB, 7 Park Place, St James's, SW1A 1LP. **Map reference** 25. **Tel.** (01) 629 7688. **Telex** 298519. **Owner** Peter de Savary. **Director** William Pound. **Open** All year. **Rooms** 11 studios, 31 suites, 1 penthouse, all with bathroom (including shower), direct-dial phone, color TV, bar. **Facilities** Elevator, library, restaurant, 24-hr. room service, secretarial facilities, bar, luggage storage and mail forwarding, small conference facilities, private dining, same day laundry and drycleaning, shoe cleaning and valeting, individual safes (but not in rooms). **Restrictions** After one visit, club membership must be sought before further stays. Club facilities are for members only. **Terms** Medium. Expensive yearly subscription. **Lunch/Dinner** Medium. Moderate fixed-price lunch menu. **Credit cards** All major cards. **Nearest tube station** Green Park, 100 yds. **Hotel parking** No. NCP in Arlington Street, SW1. **Local eating** Dukes Hotel (see p. 43); Fortnum and Mason's, Piccadilly (light snacks); Green's Champagne and Oyster Bar, 35–36 Duke Street, SW1; Suntory, 72 St James's Street, SW1; Wilton's, 55 Jermyn Street, SW1. **Local shopping** Burlington Arcade; Piccadilly stores; Burberry's, Haymarket, for raincoats; Jermyn Street for hand-made shirts. **Local interest** Royal Academy; Museum of Mankind; St James's Palace; St James's Park; Buckingham Palace.

The Savoy Hotel

Palace by the Thames

For six centuries a building named The Savoy has stood on this site overlooking the Thames. The original long-vanished palace built by Peter of Savoy, uncle to Henry III, was said in Elizabethan times to have been "the fairest manor in England." Victorian entrepreneur Richard d'Oyly Carte, discoverer of Gilbert and Sullivan, built here firstly the still-existing Savoy Theatre, for presenting the famous operettas, then in 1889 a magnificent modern hotel, luxurious beyond belief, lighted by the new electricity. To it he tempted César Ritz as manager, the famed Escoffier as chef, and American millionaires, the crowned heads of Europe, the Prince of Wales, and all the beau monde as visitors. Whistler and Monet painted the Thames from its balconies, Johann Strauss's orchestra played here; Caruso sang; Pavlova danced. In the 1920s and 30s the décor was updated and the great liners brought filmstars from Hollywood with mountains of hatboxes and cabin trunks. The first Martini in the world is said to have beeen mixed in the American Bar, meeting place of London's expatriate American community. During World War II, The Savoy achieved the dubious distinction of being London's most bombed hotel; in the post-war austerity, business slumped.

But now new life has come to the historic Savoy, whose hotel school has trained many of the world's leading managers. The vast marbled and frescoed entrance hall bustles with activity, the restaurant overlooking the Thames, where the first Pêche Melba was created for singer Nellie Melba, has been redecorated. Waiters in formal black tailcoats or gleaming white jackets whirl swiftly between tables, bearing food under domed silver covers. Afternoon tea in the Thames Foyer is justly famous – don't miss the freshly baked scones and self-indulgently creamy pastries. Some of the bedrooms have been totally refurbished, with ultra-modern fittings and bathrooms, but the magnificent Edwardian Riverside Suites still remain for the nostalgia seeker. Antique-filled, painted in pastel colors, with plasterwork picked out in white, luxurious and spacious, they make an intriguing contrast with the 1920s rooms, which retain their original marble bathrooms with massive chromium fittings and 12-inch-wide shower-heads that produce cascading tropical waterfalls. Breakfast arrives on a trolley, with starched cloth, a rose, the morning paper, and exquisite Wedgwood china. The hotel's own famous coffee, ground and vacuum-packed, may be purchased here and its own factories will make you a mattress or pair of monogrammed Irish linen sheets.

The Savoy, revered, concerned, and majestic, carries on the traditions of the stately palace that once stood here.

Opposite: dinner is laid in a sumptuous private dining room; above, mirrors and marble fireplaces evoke Edwardian elegance in the suites. Overleaf: left, the hotel from the Embankment gardens; right, one of the sitting rooms and a supremely stylish bed.

THE SAVOY HOTEL, The Strand, WC2R 0EU. **Map reference** 30. **Tel.** (01) 836 4343. **Telex** 24234. **Owners** Savoy Hotel plc. **Managing Director and General Manager** Willy Bauer. **Open** All year. **Rooms** 59 single, 85 double, 49 suites, all with bathroom (including shower), color TV, direct-dial phone, radio. **Facilities** 24-hr. room service, waiter/valet/maid service, same-day laundry/drycleaning, elevators, restaurant, grill, American Bar, Thames Foyer, 5 banqueting rooms, 8 salons, baby sitting, hotel car hire, safes, florist, ladies' and gentlemen's hairdresser, Heathrow and Southampton offices to assist arrival and departure, boutique, theater ticket desk, picnic hampers by special request. **Restrictions** None. **Terms** Medium. **Lunch/Dinner** (River Restaurant and Grill Room) Expensive. River Restaurant has medium fixed-price lunch menu and a fixed-price dinner menu which is medium Sun.–Thurs. and expensive Fri.–Sat. **Credit cards** All major cards. **Nearest tube stations** Embankment, Covent Garden, Charing Cross, Aldwych: all $\frac{1}{4}$ mile. **Hotel parking** Yes, for 500 cars. **Local eating** Boulestin, 1a Henrietta Street, WC2; Inigo Jones, 14 Garrick Street, WC2. **Local shopping** Covent Garden has numerous fashionable boutiques. **Local interest** Trafalgar Square, National Gallery and National Portrait Gallery; National Theatre, National Film Theatre, Hayward Gallery and 3 concert halls on South Bank; Inns of Court and Royal Courts of Justice; Silver Vaults in Chancery Lane; Sir John Soane's Museum, Lincoln's Inn Fields.

International renown

The Stafford is a lovely 19th-century mansion in a very quiet backwater off St James's. It has lofty public rooms embellished with ornate plasterwork, a devoted staff, many of whom have been here for anything up to 35 years, and an elaborately formal restaurant serving traditional French cooking. The menu disdains the simplicity of *nouvelle cuisine*; its dishes are rich in butter, cream, brandy, and eggs. Oysters are specially brought down from Loch Fyne, beef is from The Stafford's own Scottish herds, vegetables are perfectly cooked and served in generous helpings, desserts are deliciously rich, and everything is presented on embossed silver platters. There is even a choice of flambé dishes, served with a panache often sadly lacking elsewhere. Wines are from the hotel's deep cellars, said once to have belonged to nearby St James's Palace; beneath their whitewashed brick vaults specially-favored, often-returning guests hold occasional memorable reunions.

Manging Director Terry Holmes is the moving spirit behind the hotel. He is a Personality. His father was a porter at The Dorchester, where Terry himself served his hotel apprenticeship. Often disparagingly told that with little education and a cockney background and accent he could never hope to succeed in the hotel world, Terry delights in having been the youngest hotel managing director in the West End, the 1983/4 Chairman of the Prestige Hotel Association and the 1985 Hotelier of the Year. One of only 25 Master Hoteliers in Britain, he is a Freeman of the City of London. His friends, discovering this last honor bestowed the ancient right to drive sheep over London Bridge, produced a live one for him at a surprise party. He in turn astonished a group of guests – who happily knew him well – by leading it into their private dining room at The Stafford, and

urbanely enquiring whether they preferred their lamb on or off the bone.

The possession of a sense of humor does not indicate any absence of professionalism in Terry Holmes. Under his expert eye the hotel is immaculate, service is rapid and courteous, and nothing is overlooked or forgotten. The American Bar has a most convivial atmosphere, and is hung with trophies in the shape of pennants and caps from all over the world. There is a tiny garden terrace leading from the bar, where on summer days one may sit on the edge of the hotel's cobbled mews. Visitors relaxing from their transatlantic crossing are often to be seen enjoying the celebrated and delicious afternoon tea, which is served from silver pots and on dainty china. Nearly all the spacious bedrooms have been refurbished with fresh chintzes and their bathrooms modernized. The Stafford has its own blend not only of whisky but also of dignity, elegance, and an irresistibly warm welcome.

Opposite: the sitting room and a private dinner party in the historic cellars; above, one of the spacious bedrooms. Overleaf: left, the wine-cellars are lined with tempting vintages; right, a sitting room in one of the suites and (bottom) the welcoming American Bar.

THE STAFFORD, 16–18 St James's Place, SW1A 1NJ. **Map reference** 26. **Tel.** (01) 493 0111. **Telex** 28602. **Owners** Trafalgar House. **General Manager** Terry Holmes. **Open** All year. **Rooms** 11 single, 50 double, 5 suites, all with bathroom (including shower); color TV, and direct-dial phone. **Facilities** Dining room, restaurant, American Bar, 4 private dining rooms, Garden Terrace, elevator, hotel driver/guide available. **Restrictions** No dogs. **Terms** Medium. **Lunch/Dinner** Expensive. Medium fixed-price lunch and dinner menus. **Credit cards** All major cards. **Nearest tube station** Green Park, $\frac{1}{4}$ mile. **Hotel parking** No. NCP in Arlington Street, SW1. **Local eating** The Ritz (see p. 77); Green's Champagne and Oyster Bar, 35–36 Duke Street, SW1; Cecconi's, 5a Burlington Gardens, W1. **Local shopping** Bond Street; Piccadilly stores; Jermyn Street; Burlington Arcade; Burberry's store in Haymarket. **Local interest** St James's Palace; St James's Park; Buckingham Palace; Green Park; Royal Academy.

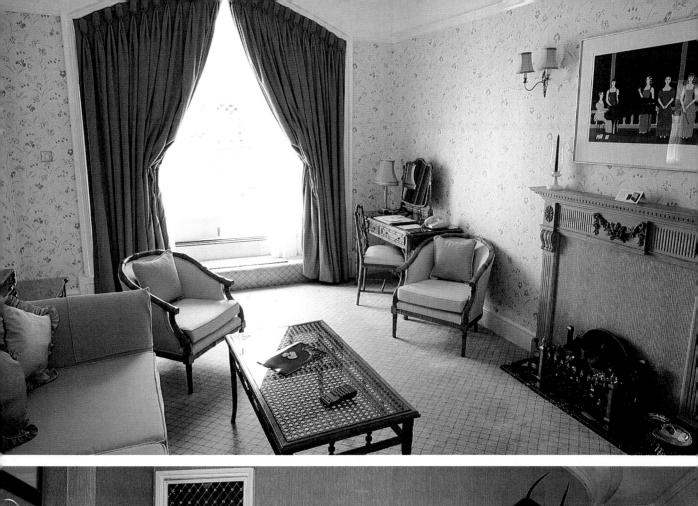

A leafy retreat

Should you be staying at The Wilderness in spring, and happen to glance out of the window of the spacious guest sitting room, you may well see a pair of wild mallards flying in to land on the lily pond where they are placidly raising their brood, such is the tranquillity of the quiet green garden.

The Hardwick family have owned land locally for many years, and The Wilderness was Charles Hardwick's boyhood home, to which 30 years ago he brought his bride from New Orleans. This stately house, built in the early 1800s, is hung with fox, hare, and badger masks (trophies of the chase), family portraits and memorabilia. Charles Hardwick's mother added the bow windows and moved the main staircase to one side, to give a view down the entrance hall into the garden, past the glass case where a stuffed fox stands with a possessive paw on a pheasant. She also furnished the magnificent yellow drawing room with antiques. The large traditional bedrooms have *en suite* modern bathrooms with showers and there are good hanging cupboards, mirrors, and plenty of books and magazines. A pair of Norwich terriers are friendly but not insistent; a stout marmalade cat is a gracious presence.

This is still a private family house, not a hotel as such, and would-be guests should write well ahead of time when planning a visit. Guests eat in their own dining room when not tempted by London restaurants. For the last eleven years meals have been cooked and served by Ana, the ebullient Spanish general factotum. I sampled with pleasure her cauliflower soup, based on good stock and perfectly seasoned, veal escalopes with fresh zucchini and new potatoes, and ripe strawberries in a Spanish liqueur. Some guests prefer total privacy, others enjoy, as I did, listening to fascinating stories of how, as recently as the lifetime of Charles Hardwick's grandfather,

stags were hunted with packs of hounds across nearby Wandsworth Common, and how Charles raised his own pack of beagles and hunted them over the family estates in Wiltshire.

In summer the Hardwicks arrange private parties for those guests attending the Wimbledon tennis tournament, with marquees on the lawn where champagne and strawberries are served. During the rest of the year, theater trips and visits to stately homes are organized for house guests.

A high wall encloses this oasis of tall trees, roses, and flowering shrubs in a quiet residential road off Wimbledon Common. It is delightful after a day in London to relax in these peaceful surroundings and contemplate with pleasure an expedition into lovely Hampshire or Sussex countryside without the prospect of London traffic to tackle.

Opposite: the house seen from the garden, over the goldfish pond where ducks nest; above, an antique chessboard table. Overleaf: left, family mementoes and trophies of the chase and (bottom) a corner of the Yellow Withdrawing Room. Right, the view of the spacious garden from the Withdrawing Room.

THE WILDERNESS, 19 Inner Park Road, Wimbledon Common, London, SW19 6ED. **Map reference** 32. **Tel.** (01) 788 3146. **Telex** No. **Owners** Charles and Shirley Hardwick. **Open** All year, except one week at Christmas. **Rooms** 3 doubles (1 with four-poster), 1 with own bathroom, 2 with shared bathroom. Both bathrooms have a shower. **Facilities** Large private sitting room, private dining room, ¾-acre garden. **Restrictions** No dogs; no children under 10. **Terms** Moderate; English breakfast included. **Lunch** No. **Dinner** (by arrangement only; fixed price) Medium. **Credit cards** American Express. **Nearest tube station** Southfields, ½ mile (but Wimbledon, 1 mile, is more attractive). **Hotel parking** Yes. **Local eating** Yesterday, 12–14 Leopold Road, SW19; other restaurants as suggested by hosts. **Local interest** Wimbledon Lawn Tennis Club (All-England Tennis Championships are last week in June and first week in July); Richmond Park, the Royal Botanical Gardens at Kew, Hampton Court palace, and Wisley Royal Horticultural Society Gardens are all a short drive away.

Four London Clubs

Traditions upheld

London Clubs are bastions of tradition. With great reluctance they have allowed ladies in through their discreet portals, even then closely confining them to certain areas, except of course in the Women's Clubs. Housed in mansions, to which they progressed after their first informal beginnings in London's coffee houses in the 18th century, they are groups of like-minded people with a common interest or background. There is an annual subscription. Charges thereafter are rather reasonable, since the clubs are non-profit-making, and are paid as incurred. Club servants are never tipped, members donating instead to a staff fund. Many clubs are by their very nature exclusively British, but The Oxford and Cambridge Club, Caledonian Club, American Club, and University Women's Club have members all over the world. They serve mainly as meeting places, but all these four also have some accommodation, as simple and basic as the other parts of the premises are palatial. They also have very grand dining rooms, serving traditional British food.

You must be a graduate of one of the two universities in order to belong to The Oxford and Cambridge Club. It has dignified premises, built in 1834, on Pall Mall, which include a library – where (if a man) you can eat toasted teacakes in deep leather chairs – squash courts, and a Ladies' Wing. The Caledonian Club's members must be of Scottish descent – no further back than a grandparent – or have served in a Scottish regiment, or have done some service for, or have close association with, Scotland. The imposing mansion on Halkin Street in Belgravia has tartans, claymores, and paintings of Highland scenes in evidence, haggis on the menu, and several gentlemen-only areas. The American Club on Piccadilly, overlooking Green Park, is in an 1883 building containing fine 18th-century overmantles

from a previous house on this site. Ladies have finally been admitted with full status. U.S. citizenship, or close connections with the U.S.A., are required for membership.

The University Women's Club has its centenary year in 1986. The lovely house on Audley Square, just off Park Lane, was built in 1870 and belonged to the Russell family, whose crest is over the dining-room fireplace. It was for many years a salon, where leading political and intellectual figures of the time met to exchange ideas. Subsequently, it became a club which was a rallying point for the pioneers of women's education in England. Women university graduates from all over the world receive a warm welcome; equivalent qualifications or intellectual eminence can also make one eligible for membership.

To belong to a Club one must be elected by its members, and respect its traditions, conventions, and formality. Similar clubs abroad have reciprocal arrangements with these clubs, a useful point for visitors to England to check before leaving home. English residents may find a London Club a most convenient and agreeable London base.

Opposite: top, the dignified library in the University Women's Club; bottom left, one of The Oxford and Cambridge Club's stately staircases; bottom right, a stag's head dominates the stairs in The Caledonian Club. The American Club has a dining room overlooking Green Park (above) and a gracious staircase (overleaf).

THE UNITED OXFORD AND CAMBRIDGE UNIVERSITY CLUB, 71 Pall Mall, SW1. **Map reference 28. Tel.** (01) 930 5151. **Membership Secretary** D. F. Gwynne. **Facilities** Smoking room, coffee room, library, squash courts, squash bar, ladies' wing, elevator. **Rooms** 26 single, 13 double, all with private bathroom, including tub or shower, and tel. THE CALEDONIAN CLUB, 9 Halkin Street, SW1X 7DR. **Map reference 8. Tel.** (01) 235 5162/6. **Secretary** Commander C. M. Bagguley, R.N. **Facilities** Drawing room, bar, dining room. **Rooms** 19 single, 12 double, all with bathroom including tub or shower. THE AMERICAN CLUB, 95

Piccadilly, W1V 0BS. **Map reference 15. Tel.** (01) 499 2303. **Admin. Secretary** Mrs Linda Pailthorpe. **Facilities** 2 drawing rooms, 2 dining rooms. **Rooms** 3 double, separate bathrooms with showers. THE UNIVERSITY WOMEN'S CLUB, 2 Audley Square, South Audley Street, W1Y 6DB. **Map reference 17. Tel.** (01) 499 6478/2268. **Club Secretary** Mrs Elizabeth Hord. **Facilities** Library, drawing room, dining room, elevator. **Rooms** 18 single, 6 double. Separate bathrooms. Details of membership qualifications and dues of all four clubs on application.